D0122535

Cricket Conversations

Peter Walker

talks with

Gary Sobers
Ray Illingworth
Barry Richards
Tom Cartwright
Roy Fredericks
Greg Chappell
Mike Procter
Bishen Bedi
Alan Knott
Glenn Turner
Basil d'Oliveira
Majid Khan
Brian Close

Foreword by JOHN ARLOTT

PELHAM BOOKS LONDON

First published in Great Britain by
PELHAM BOOKS LTD
52 Bedford Square
London WC1B 3EF

1978

Photographs by Patrick Eagar

ISBN O 7207 1047 2

Printed in Great Britain by Hollen Street Press, Slough
Bound by J.M. Dent, Letchworth
Typeset by Saildean Limited, Kingston, Surrey.

To Sarah, Justin and Daniel:
'Look, listen and learn'

Contents

Foreword

by John Arlott

In the past three years Peter Walker's Sunday teatime interview on BBC 2 has become one of the most original and absorbing items of sport broadcasting. As every professional interviewer knows it is not easy to fill a quarter-of-an-hour period with the talk of a specialist who is not an experienced broadcaster. Only a man who is himself an expert in that speciality, and that specialist among professional broadcasters, a good interviewer, can do that.

There are several types of interview: the 'celebrity' who uses his interviewee to express his own personality; the 'Oh, I say, isn't that lovely' type who skims meaninglessly over the surface, discovering nothing and leaving his 'subject' a two-dimensional figure; his opposite, the aggressor who seeks to expose and destroy his victim; and, ultimately, the true – midwife – interviewer, interested, seeking to know more about the person with him, drawing him out. There is a good interview in everyone; but it needs a good interviewer to extract it. Peter Walker has become a highly practised interviewer, capable of a sound job in most fields but none so good as on cricket, because his knowledge of the game is so deep that often he plumbs unexpected depths in his interviewee.

Unknowingly, and in many respects fortuitously, he prepared for this aspect of the media on several levels. Born in England, he was brought up and educated in South Africa. He was a good games player with a literary home background. From 1950 until his death in 1965, Peter's father was drama critic of *The Star* newspaper in Johannesburg and so he grew up in an atmosphere of the arts. In 1954, when Peter was eighteen, he came to Britain and went to the Glamorgan cricket headquarters at Cardiff for a trial which so impressed Wilfred Wooller – with whom he has enjoyed a love-hate relationship ever since – that he was at once taken on the ground staff.

In his career he enjoyed most of the successes open to an English cricketer. A stylish batsman with an air of ease and fine hitting power, he bowled both orthodox slow left arm and 'Trevor Goddard style' medium pace over the wicket and was a close fieldsman without peer. He performed the cricketer's double of a thousand runs and a hundred wickets – plus 73 catches – in a season; won three England Test caps, and the reputation of being one of the two or three finest short leg fieldsmen in history. Yet, if he had taken the game more seriously, he might have gone even further.

Of course he took it seriously – no man plays international cricket who treats it lightly – but his mind and interests were too wide for him to regard it as singlemindedly as most who make high reputations in it. Resolved not to lose his sense of proportion, or to forget that it is only a game, he could sometimes stand back and laugh about it. At others, it tortured him. As a bowler he could be so beset by nerves, when he was trying his hardest, that he lost both length and line. Another day, after he had 'given it away', he would idle up and bowl perfectly. At short leg he fielded suicidally close; imaginative enough to be frightened; determined enough not to flinch; quick enough to move for a ball that crucial fraction of a second faster than the average man; light and lengthy enough in body, telescopic enough in arm, and prehensile enough of hand, to make some bewildering catches. In his three Tests – all against South Africa in 1960 – he was sent in too low and bowled too little; he did not fail but he had no real chance to succeed as an all-rounder. Two years afterwards he announced that he was leaving county cricket and went back to South Africa. After a season with

Western Province, though, he returned next spring to Glamorgan and played for them for another decade before he finally retired. The respect in which his fellow players held him was reflected in his election as Chairman of the Cricketers' Association.

All this time he had been occupied with the media. The happy knack of being able to ad lib fluently brought him broadcasting in several capacities for BBC Wales. He wrote for the press, never more impressively than in interview-type features which frequently were strikingly revealing of their subject. He soon became established, too, on Welsh television. To its own benefit and those of its performers and audience, Welsh broadcasting – in both sound and vision – is what the English tend to call parochial when, in fact, it is truly national, and generally satisfying to those concerned. Alun Williams, Cliff Morgan and Peter Walker have come out also onto the stage of British broadcasting.

Peter Walker had served a thorough apprenticeship in Wales before he took over from Frank Bough as 'front man' for the John Player Sunday League cricket broadcasts on BBC 2. When he was given the opportunity to conduct a teatime interview he was keen enough and modest enough not to realize he had made an instant success. He studies his subject in advance; not to air his knowledge, but in order to ask the right initial questions until they open up the deeper questions – and the answers – which were not available in the background reading. It is the interviewing of an informed and interested questioner; and the results printed here show it to be sound and human and with all the surprise of spontaneous talk.

Preface

Books by and about cricket and cricketers probably fill as much space on library bookshelves as any two other sports combined. There's something about it and the people who inhabit the rarefied first-class-cricket atmosphere of this most English of games that is endlessly fascinating.

My own experience at Test match level was short but in no way less memorable for me because of its briefness. They talk of the loneliness of the long-distance runner, yet nothing could be more solitary than my standing waiting to receive my first ball in the first Test against South Africa at Edgbaston in 1960. Far away in the distance pawing the ground stood Neil Adcock, then one of the fastest bowlers in the world. Our close friendship developed in the league in Johannesburg was a thing of the past!

The men who play regularly at international level are a complex mix. The extroverted, uninhibited batting of West Indian Viv Richards contrasts strongly with his off-the-field personality – diffident, thoughtful and very much the 'small island' man. Others, like Geoff Boycott, play cricket in the same way they approach life: hard, introverted and uncompromising.

Neither appears in this book. Not because they are unworthy of a place on merit; far from it. Both would almost certainly feature in a current World Eleven. But there are others with whom I have come in contact over a period of twenty-four years in first-class cricket who frankly have a more unexpected and therefore surprising view on the game and how they approach it.

The idea for this book goes back to 1971, when I did a short series of cricketing profiles for the *Guardian* newspaper. Some of these I have revamped and updated, drawing in thoughts and information from subsequent conversations with the players concerned. Others I have virtually left as they originally were because, with the benefit of hindsight, a man's beliefs at any one moment in his development become of historical interest. The remainder are a spin-off from the teatime interviews I've conducted over the past three years as part of my role as the linkman for BBC 2's John Player Sunday League programme. These conversations on a cricketer-to-cricketer basis, before an audience of three million plus, usually last around seventeen minutes between the innings but often continue long after play has ended.

With the ever-increasing exposure of cricket in the media, the fanfares and raspberries that greet success and failure growing ever louder and the 1977 bombshell of Kerry Packer, it's hardly surprising that some of the game's leading exponents have developed withdrawal symptoms from anyone connected with radio, television and the press. I believe, with suitable modesty, that my actually having been in the kitchen where the heat is hottest has enabled me to break down the natural caution these international cricketers might otherwise have felt.

I hope you feel this way too.

Peter Walker

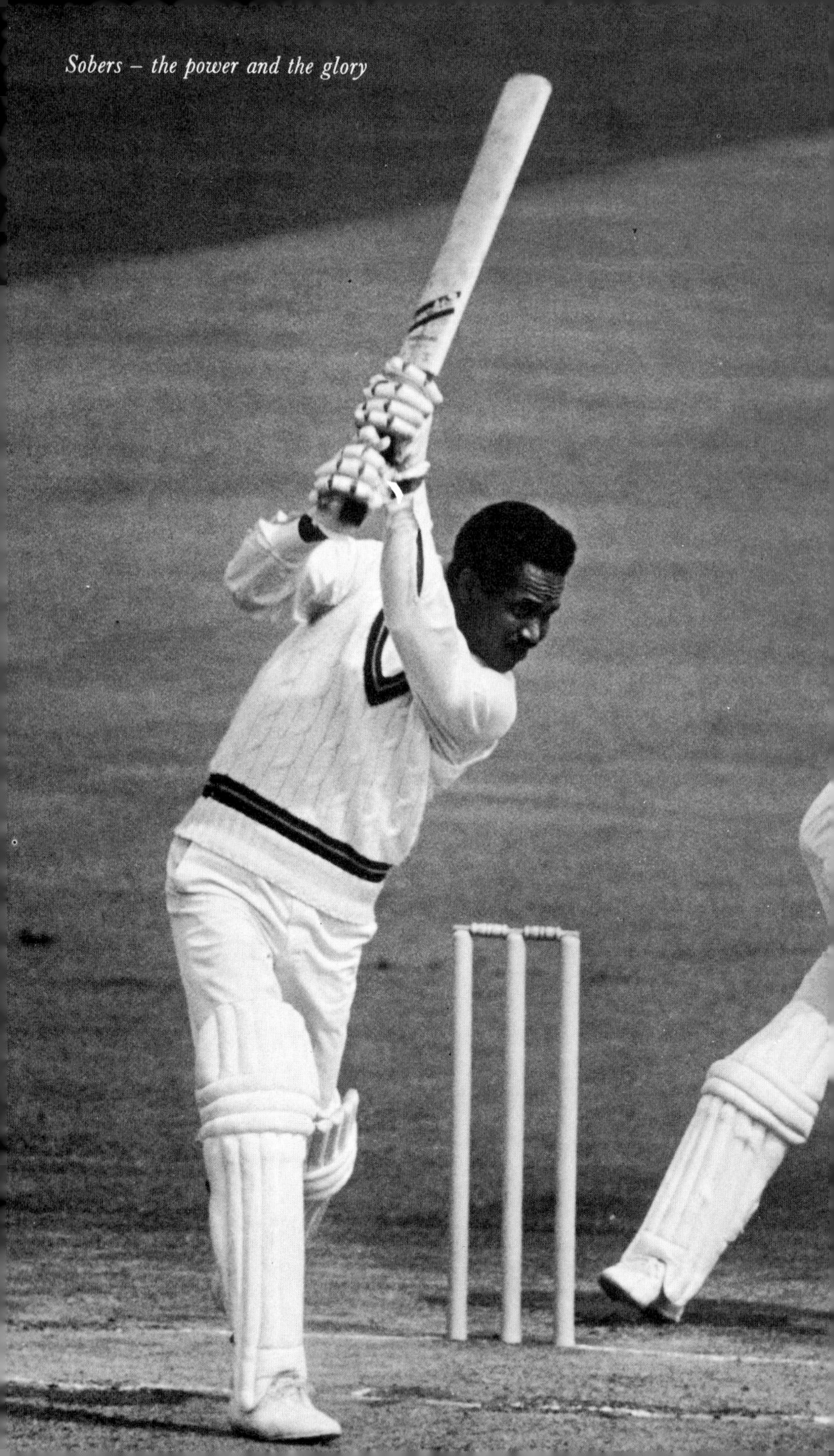

Sobers – the power and the glory

Gary Sobers

Most of the cricketers in this book are currently still in the first-class game. An exception is Gary Sobers. But then he's been an exception to all the rules since cricketing history began. To my mind he is the greatest all-round cricketer that has ever lived. If I want confirmation of this I need turn only to people like Illingworth, Snow, Cowdrey, Bedi, Majid, the Chappell brothers, Lillee, Barry Richards and Procter. 'Sobey' is their choice too.

The man not only had everything, he had it in abundance. A superb striker of the ball, he was also a supreme technician on a bad wicket, a rarity in a player brought up away from the day-to-day varying challenges of English pitches. A bowler who could go through the full spectrum of deliveries from genuinely fast – his bouncer was said to be quicker than Wes Hall's – to variations of swing both ways, right down to spin. Even here there was variety. Either the genuine orthodox slow-left-hand variety or a mixture of offbreaks and difficult-to-pick googlies. As a close fielder he must be ranked as one of the best there has ever been.

Now there are a number of Test-class all-rounders who command international respect. Trevor Bailey, Alan Davidson and Ritchie Benaud come readily to mind. But only Sobers qualified for inclusion in any World Eleven of his time as a specialist performer in all three categories of the game.

It will hardly surprise anyone who saw Gary play that he was born with five fingers, not four, on each hand! Everything he did on the field was just that little bit more accomplished than the other twenty-one. No one playing today looks remotely likely to break his aggregate of 7627 runs in Test cricket. It will take a superman to top his individual innings record of 365 against Pakistan in 1958, and after a hundred years of first-class cricket he remains the only man ever to hit six sixes in an over. I was privileged to be there on that occasion. Gary had come in to bat at Swansea in the summer of 1968 during the period he spent with Nottinghamshire in the English County Championship. He had reached forty after half an hour at the crease, and with Nottinghamshire looking for quick runs before declaring, it was Malcolm Nash who ran up to bowl the first ball of what was to be the historic over.

Two things need to be said of the events which followed. There was no conscious effort by Gary to go for a world record because, typical of the man and his attitude to such things, he had no idea what the existing best was! Secondly, Malcolm Nash, normally a medium-pace swing bowler, was experimenting at that time with a brand of slow left-hand spinners.

But having said this for the defence, the prosecuting bat of Sobers not only won the case but created a timeless moment in cricket, because fortunately for posterity the over was recorded by BBC Wales television cameras which were covering the game for domestic consumption.

I stood at first slip as the first two balls of indifferent length and direction were dispatched far over the leg-side boundary wall with that characteristic flaying yet graceful arc of his bat. The third was a classic straight drive to a full-length ball that landed some thirty yards up the concrete members' enclosure embankment at St Helens, Swansea. While the ball was being retrieved, Eifion Jones, the Glamorgan wicketkeeper, jokingly said to Gary: 'I bet you can't hit the next three for six!' The essence of fun and the huge enjoyment of a challenge were very visible parts of Sobers' personality. Whether or not he lost his wicket that day was totally immaterial.

Away went the fourth ball, also short and down the legside. The fifth was headed in the same direction as number three but slightly mishit, and it fell to earth on the boundary edge where it was held by Roger Davis, who sprawled across the line for it to count as another six.

Sobers' wind-up for the last ball is one of the most indelible memories I retain from my eighteen years as a first-class cricketer. Nash, abandoning all pretensions of trying to either spin or flight the ball, tried a fast seamer. But in the process he pulled it short, and Sobers, with a catapulting pivot, hooked the ball way over the scoreboard out of the ground down a neighbouring road, and I'm almost prepared to swear that it pitched just short of the Swansea Guildhall a mile away! That last blow wasn't a six, it was a twelve!

Like all who played with and against him, my recollections of Gary Sobers are numbered amongst my cricketing riches. To have lived in the same era is a privilege, to have known and talked to the man an experience to be treasured. Never was genius more human.

To be sure there were moments when the sheer weight of public adulation and the invasion of his private life proved an irksome burden, but amongst his own kind the man was a genuinely unaffected charmer.

I first met him in the summer of his first visit to Britain with the 1957 West Indians when, as a twenty-one-year-old who had already made his Test debut three years previously, he scored over 1600 runs and took 37 wickets in a country where very few make any impression on their first tour. In those days before Sunday cricket came into being I played regularly for a charity showbiz eleven organized by that good-hearted cricketing 'nut' Vic Lewis. One Sunday we met a good-class London team. Sobers and his great friend Collie Smith (a year later to die tragically in a car crash with Sobers at the wheel) were late in arriving from the north, where they were both playing as professionals in the Lancashire League. I opened the batting on one of the greenest, most difficult wickets I've ever played on. I lasted three balls and by the time the two West Indians had arrived at the ground we were 16 for 6! However, the eventual declaration came at 172 for 7, Sobers not out 153, after providing the most dazzling exhibition of batting skill I have ever seen.

In his prime, Sobers personified all the best things in West Indian cricket. The instinct to attack the bowling, the superb feline grace that seems genetic in the people of the Caribbean, and the broad, ready smile never far from the surface. But what Sobers did in his cricketing lifetime was to add a new dimension to the inherent skills of his countrymen. Enormously influenced by the late Sir Frank Worrell, Sobers continued and built on the foundations laid by Sir Frank, putting a rod of steel into West Indian performances in adversity. Up to this period no one had ever questioned their ability as individuals, but as a team under pressure? Well, that was a different matter. This characteristic may well have been true prior to Worrell and Sobers but is most certainly not so today, even allowing for a momentary relapse during their tour of Australia in 1975/6.

Like many West Indians, Sobers profited greatly from his stay in the Lancashire Leagues where the mainly amateur team's success is often dependent on their pro's performance. As a result of his years in the north, Sobers never did anything other than lead from the front, and although critics were often nonplussed by his decision to bat as low as number 6 or even 7 in the West Indies Test team, few really appreciated the enormous drain on the man in his multiple role as captain and three-in-one bowler.

As he got older, the spark needed more vigorous fanning before bursting into flame. But always, when the occasion demanded it, he could produce the goods almost to the same Herculean level as in the Lords Test match in 1966 when, with the West Indies leading England by a mere nine runs with five of their second innings wickets gone, Sobers and his cousin, the inexperienced David Holford, added 268 for the fifth wicket; Sobers 163, Holford 105, a partnership which not only saved West Indies from defeat but so nearly snatched them an impossible victory on the last day.

For someone who takes such great pride in being a West Indian, Sobers is a man who has made some odd, controversial decisions which got him into hot water at home. In 1970 he captained the Rest of the World side against England. His team included five South Africans. He then went to Rhodesia for two days and played in a double-wicket multiracial competition. This decision caused an uproar in the Caribbean and almost led to the cancellation of the Indian tour of 1971. The furore he caused hastened his departure from the international scene, and although greatly troubled in his latter years with niggling shoulder and knee injuries, there is no doubt in my mind that in 1974 Sobers retired at least two years before he needed to.

Fortunately the tremendous service and dedication he put into cricket quickly washed away the bitterness, and his knighthood by the Queen during her tour of the West Indies in February 1975 was universally welcomed and applauded.

To many, Sobers the man remains something of an enigma. Behind the expansive smile, the ready West Indian sense of humour, lies a complex character, someone who often in his playing days was unsure of his own incredible abilities. Yet he was unswerving in his views on the overlapping roles and inter-relationship between sport and politics. In spite of his rolling-shouldered, loose-limbed carriage on the field, which suggested a certain lack of total commitment, Sobers was a cricketer with a strong sense of realism and outspoken views on the way the game should be played. But although he was a fierce competitor on the field he rarely lost his 'cool', backing instead his ability to overcome his opponent.

Who could doubt this judgement? A hypothetical question is sometimes posed. 'Who would you like to play an innings if your life depended on it?' I have no doubt whom I would pick. Sir Garfield St Aubrun Sobers. He is the only man I have ever played against who, if I overheard him say before the start of an innings that he was going to get a hundred, would make me reach for a phone to contact the nearest bookmaker!

Sobers' was a talent apart, he was a man who so raised the excitement level of people watching that the progress of the game itself became secondary. He hit the ball with a full-flowing swing that was so fast that even a ball struck well away from the middle of the bat still flew to the boundary. Fielding in the covers to Sobers one always stood twenty feet deeper than for other mortals. When he was bowling, one never ever felt secure or completely sure what kind of ball he was going to deliver.

Off the field, Gary was a good mixer, and there are many conversations over the period of about six years which I noted in my diary and which could now be developed. But I prefer to recall one in particular. It was in 1971, a difficult time for Sobers, when he seemed at war with the whole administration of West Indian cricket and the period when knee and shoulder troubles were beginning to eat into those matchless skills.

He had been playing cricket around the world virtually non-stop for the previous ten years. On this particular occasion it had been a long hard day in the field for Nottinghamshire, the team he was then captaining. The crowd, like the sunshine, had been sparse and his luck on the horses that day hadn't been too good. We sat in a back bar behind the pavilion at Trent Bridge while outside twenty young autograph hunters waited for him to come out. The greatest cricketer the world has ever seen unwound as I opened the batting. What he had stored up inside him later moved Sir Neville Cardus to say that he at last understood this most complex of men.

'Poetry in motion'

WALKER: Knowing how taxing an English county season can be, the thing which both impresses and amazes me is how you keep going for almost twelve months of the year, year in year out, without any apparent loss of form or interest.
SOBERS: I think it's because I get so much pleasure out of playing the game at all levels right up from charity exhibition matches to a Test series. For instance, I was playing out in Barbados seven days before the beginning of the English season. To me, there's so much to get from the game, so many new things to try, that I never get bored. Take bowling. I'm a great believer that the ball does the work. Different balls require a different approach. Some swing or spin, some don't. I'm always changing my grip or angle of delivery trying to find what will make the ball respond. I think a lot of baloney is talked about the technique of bowling; getting your wrist, shoulder and arm into the right position and so on. To me the state, if you like 'character', of the ball is the decisive thing.
WALKER: In this country there's a tendency among critics to describe the West Indian style or attitude as natural and uninhibited. Having played against you many times I would say that shorn of your individual flourish you've a sound, carefully-worked-out batting technique. Is this true?
SOBERS: Certainly. The way I strike the ball could be called 'my unconscious style' but I'm very aware of getting the basics right. Being objective, I think I pick up the flight of the ball quicker than most players. To me the most important thing in batting is moving my feet immediately to get behind the line of the ball. Playing forward or back isn't really important to me, particularly against pace bowling – I tend to follow the swing or play at the ball more than most English players, who tend to get locked into one set stroke. For instance, I could start playing at the ball as it's on the way, intending, say, to hit it straight back past the bowler. If it moves away from me in the air I'll adjust in mid-stroke to hit it through the covers or even cut it if it really swings a lot. While I remember, thinking back to your first question, I've been accused,

particularly in 1969, of having played too much cricket and being stale. That's nonsense. I don't believe players get stale. What happens is they get physically tired and lose a bit of their keenness, that's all.

WALKER: How aware of your position inside the game are you – or if you like, your reputation? Are you conscious that each time you go on to the field you're expected to show not only the crowd but also your fellow cricketers that you are in fact 'the greatest'?

SOBERS: Obviously I know what's expected of me and I'm lucky in a way that I'm a compulsive trier, whatever the state of the game. This means that whatever talent I've got will always be expressed through my own hundred-per-cent endeavours. I wouldn't be honest if I said that I was unaware that mine is an ability out of the ordinary. I know it is and shall always be grateful for it. I like to think, however, that mine is a humble awareness. For instance, I rarely get upset by the efforts or failings of inferior players in my team. I find cricket an immensely taxing game. What must it be like for them?

What does rile me, however, is when a good player fails to make use of his ability – like Colin Cowdrey, when he's obsessed by playing bat and pad. But what a player he becomes when he sheds this sort of inhibition! From my point of view I won't attempt anything which I don't think I can do capably. I'm very self-conscious about the possibility of making a fool of myself. That's why I'm not bowling wrist spinners at this stage of the season. I haven't the confidence to 'drop' them at the moment, and until I get in the nets to work at it I won't use them in a match.

WALKER: Just how often do you practise?

SOBERS: Rarely, if ever. I reckon one uses up too much energy in the nets. I can hardly remember the last time I practised batting and the only bowling I do try to perfect in the nets is, as I said, wrist spinners. I'm playing in so many proper matches that to me practice is a waste of time and on the few occasions I've had, say, a couple of months off I've found it quite simple to slip back into the groove.

WALKER: I don't suppose any cricketer has ever had so many accolades heaped upon him, and deserved ones they are, but there have been moments where your actions have brought severe criticism: your attitude to playing with and against cricketers from Rhodesia and South Africa and also – and this might be related – there have been questions about Gary Sobers being the right person to captain the West Indies.

SOBERS: First, the criticism of my captaincy. This always happens back home if we lose a Test or a series, as we did recently against India. Then there was a call in some quarters, particularly in Trinidad, for Joey Carew to be given my job. I'll tell you frankly, this sort of criticism, or for that matter criticism generally, doesn't worry me, and I certainly don't take any notice of it; I'm just as wary of too much praise. In the West Indies in particular, the people who do the loudest shouting know the least about the game. I'll talk and debate cricket with anyone whose knowledge I respect or who has an inquiring interest, but I've no time for 'camp followers' and people who are destructive without any real understanding of the game.

As to my attitude to apartheid and cricket, I'm one who first of all believes in owing an allegiance to my friends, not to political ideals. I captained the Rest of the World team in England last year which had five South Africans – Richards, Barlow, Procter and the two Pollocks – in the side. We got on very well and when they asked me if I'd play for them in a special competition in Rhodesia, I agreed. There was a great deal of pressure on me back in the West Indies not to go and to dissociate myself from the South African tour of the UK, which in any event never came off. Whatever you or anyone else feels about the situation, I stand firmly in the camp of the 'bridge builders', and as far as I am concerned I'll be ready to play against South Africans, whatever their colour, any time it is felt that the cause of cricket is being promoted. Obviously, I am anti-apartheid, but I reserve the right to tackle the problem of breaking it in my own way. Surely if I can play in competition with white South Africans and do better than them, then this is a clear indication to the politicians out there that people of all colours can and should compete on equal terms.

WALKER: In a career lasting eighteen years you have crammed more into life than most complete teams! You've made more money out of cricket than anyone else before. But have you managed to make the future secure once you leave the game?

SOBERS: Not as secure as it might be. Before I got married I led a pretty full social life and it is no secret I enjoy a flutter on the horses. Yes, I've made a lot of money out of the game – not a vast sum by comparison with some in other professional sports, and I must say I have been disappointed by a great deal of the financial advice and so-called guidance I have been given. Because of this I'm now a lot more wary, perhaps cynical, of people who come up offering this sort of help and suggestion. But at the moment I live very well, though the future outside the game is just beginning to concern me.

WALKER: How do you see your immediate future?

SOBERS: Well, I reckon I've got three more years in the game – that takes me up to the end of my present contract with Nottinghamshire. Physically I don't feel any different now from when I was twenty-five; in fact, I reckon I have been at my peak for the past ten years. This coming winter I'll probably go out to Adelaide for the Australian season. I promised them I'd go back once more before I retire. But when I eventually give up playing, I'll certainly miss county cricket. You know the English press and public greatly undervalue the quality of their own players. Outside the current England team I can think of literally tens of cricketers whom I 'rate'; Cartwright, Nash, Pocock, Allen, Smedley, Pilling, Page – I could go on for half an hour reeling names off. These are very good players – in the £100,000 footballer class, if you like.

WALKER: When you do eventually give up active cricket, what do you hope to do?

SOBERS: I am not really sure. I've hardly needed to do anything else but play cricket since I was eighteen. But something in the government service back home in the West Indies would suit me fine. England's too cold in the winter and Australia's too far. But whatever it is I must be free to express myself in my own way, just as I have always attempted to do on the cricket field. Please don't shut me away indoors somewhere. Who knows, there might be a new 'Sobers' in the backstreets of Bridgetown, Barbados. In a strange, rather selfish way I'd like to be the one who finds him and presents him to the people.

Stand and deliver

Ray Illingworth

By any standards, the career of Ray Illingworth has been a successful and varied one. Yet it needed a personal crisis within Yorkshire to free him from the often stifling atmosphere of English cricket's leading county. Had not Yorkshire stood firm in 1968 and refused his demand for a long-term contract – long-term in cricket being three years – then Illingworth would in all probability have finished his career with them, retired to a pub in Pudsey or nearby, and been remembered as an in-and-out international cricketer without quite the ability to retain a regular place.

Yorkshire's short-sightedness then, although they have since eaten humble pie by inviting him back to take up a position as team manager as from 1979, proved Leicestershire's and England's long-term gain. Indeed, there were many supporters of the White Rose county who questioned their committee's judgement that at the then age of thirty-seven Ray Illingworth had precious little to offer Yorkshire.

History was to show that his greatest contributions were still to come.

The other day I was running my eye through a benefit brochure produced to coincide with Illingworth's 1977 testimonial season. Naturally enough it is filled with complimentary articles about what a fine fellow Raymond is, little

Illingworth – the 'old fox' on the hunt

anecdotes about the man, and detailed statistics covering his first-class career, which began in 1951 with just a single innings of 56 against Hampshire and no turn at the bowling crease. In the twenty-six years that have followed he's scored nearly 24,000 runs, taken 2000 wickets and held 400 catches, an impressive record indeed. But what particularly interested me were the comments by leading players about his captaincy.

Richie Benaud: 'The best captain I ever played against in Test cricket was Peter May. The best captain I never played against in Test cricket was Ray Illingworth. He stands very high in my list of cricketers in the twenty-nine years I have been playing or watching the game.' Jim Laker: 'Illingworth's greatest strength has been that as captain of both England and Leicestershire he has always commanded the deepest respect of every player. They would do anything for him.' Alan Knott: 'He's the best captain I've ever played under. With Ray you don't have to wait long to discover that he's truly brilliant under pressure.' Geoff Boycott: 'I rate Illy along with Brian Close as the best captain I ever played under. He's without doubt one of the most knowledgeable professional cricketers I have ever known.' Ken Barrington: 'He's one of the most remarkable cricketers of our time – a strategic genius with a first-class cricket brain. I am not alone in hoping that when the time comes for him to end his illustrious career, his astute tactical brain will continue to serve English cricket in other directions. To allow such rare talent and wide experience to drift out of the game would be crass folly.' John Snow: 'His captaincy is based on logic, not guesswork. We share a dislike of losing. To captain a fast bowler one needs instinct and, not least, a degree of psychology. Ray has this in abundance and I found him an easy person to associate with and play under, a fact which helped me a great deal, particularly in Australia.'

All of these quotes refer specifically to Illingworth's ability as a leader of men. His place in cricketing history centres on this factor more than on his considerable playing skills.

I've been trying to analyse in my mind what it is that makes a good captain and, in Illingworth's case, an exceptional one.

Not much can be done when your side is batting, a point which reinforces my belief that the finest captains have nearly always been bowlers, or at least batsmen who can bowl a bit. One third part of captaincy is in knowing the mental make-up of your bowlers, one third relates to reading batsmen and knowing what sort of fields to place for them and the other third is all about putting pressure on the opposition. Illingworth scores very high marks in all three departments. His handling of John Snow in Australia in 1971 turned a talented but difficult-to-control human being into one of the most consistently hostile strike weapons ever to play for England. With the departure of Illingworth from the international scene in 1973, Snow's career at this level also took a nosedive. It is said that only Illingworth could bring the best out of Snow, and the facts seem to back this assertion. Together, with help from Knott, Underwood & Co., they brought back the Ashes from Australia in 1971, in the process of becoming the only England side ever to go through a series out there undefeated.

This last word gives a clue to the heart of Illingworth's philosophy about captaincy. An honourable draw in Yorkshire carries almost as much prestige as a convincing win. Battles on the retreat are fought step by step, they never become a disintegrating farce. But it can work the other way, and one of the more regularly aired criticisms of his leadership is his inherent northern caution, with the emphasis on containment rather than attack. Yet no one who has been on the receiving end of Illingworth's skill, either as a bowler or captain, is ever less than wholly aware that a momentary lapse will be instantly seized upon and the newly gained advantage vigorously pressed home.

An expressive, articulately emphatic companion off the field, Illingworth's presence on it is laconic and disciplined. Yorkshire cricket breeds a special gene into its sons which I've rarely come across in others. It gives them 'presence' in the authoritative sense, commanding respect and obedience.

Few question Illingworth's decisions on the field, yet he is not above receiving suggestions or advice. An autocrat without the manner, a disciplinarian without being bombastic, the respect the Leicester and former England captain on thirty-six occasions in his fourteen years as an international player receives from his fellow players is remarkable and provides the pass key into his longevity in this most demanding of roles.

Illingworth has always been a 'player's man'. After he took over as captain of England in 1969, the side went twenty-two games before being defeated, their longest-ever run. Under him the talents of Knott, Willis, Amiss, Underwood and the precocious Greig blossomed. It was Illingworth who, on behalf of his players, challenged the system over payment of expenses; Illingworth who insisted on the right sort of medical and physiotherapy advice accompanying his team on overseas tours; Illingworth who accepted the brunt of criticisms of his team following a bad day. Privately there would be individual comment, even chastisement, but in public the Yorkshireman led with his own chin. Because of this and his obvious pride in his own and everyone else's performance, cricketers, whatever their county, quickly fell in behind his banner. Even though he has been out of the international scene for five years and is nearer fifty than forty, his name was seriously put forward as a possible captain of the Rest of the World team in the Kerry Packer series in Australia!

It is his unifying qualities that make him such a natural captain. A first-class county dressing-room where a dozen or so professional cricketers are mixed together in a tight knot during the four-month English season can be a volatile cockpit. Leicestershire's quite incredible success since Illingworth joined them in 1968 is a product of careful player employment, notably by Michael Turner, their youthful secretary/manager who was principally behind the engagement of Illingworth after his disagreement with Yorkshire, forthright planning by an energetic committee who correctly give Turner and their captain their heads, and Illingworth's talent to turn a hotchpotch of players, many of them other counties' rejects, into one single-minded unit.

Although Leicestershire was founded in 1879 it took ninety-three years before they won anything. Under Illingworth they triumphed in the 1972 Benson & Hedges Cup, a feat repeated in 1975 after losing in the 1974 final. They also finished top of the pile in the 1974 and 1977 John Player League and won the most coveted prize of all, the County Championship, in 1975!

From once being the pushovers of the county circuit, Leicestershire are now among the most feared teams in the land, with a combination of individuals capable of winning the most testing examination of skills, the County Championship as well as the explosive 40-over Sunday League.

With the exception of Fred Trueman, Yorkshire cricketers are not renowned for their sense of humour. The game – and life itself – is a serious, often desperate matter, not to be joked about. Rare is the tyke who can tell a cricketing joke against himself, and until recent years Raymond Illingworth was an archetypal Yorkshireman.

Which leads me back to my opening paragraph. In his early days with Yorkshire there were few more consistently complaining members of the team than he. His complaints were not of a vicious feud-making type, but the recriminations and the impression he gave that everything and everyone was against him gave Ray a reputation for negativeness and unsociability.

Relationships between the Yorkshire playing staff and their committee go through periodical upheavals. Since the war one remembers the cases of Wardle, Trueman, Close, and Illingworth, plus innumerable other less well-known cricketers, all of whom eventually left the county for less acrimonious pastures and became integral parts of other county teams.

Illingworth needed Leicestershire almost as much as they needed him. The hunting county brought out a more compassionate, comprehending side to his nature. They gave him the sense of security and importance that he had been consistently denied even during his halcyon days with Yorkshire. In return, with greater personal freedom, he warmed as a person and with the responsibility of captaincy, first of his county and then suddenly of his country when Cowdrey was injured, he became a more outgoing creature with a newly developed facet of his personality blossoming, care and concern for his players.

A great deal of credit for this change, remarkable in a mature man of such previously fixed views, must go to the most able administrator in English cricket, the Leicestershire secretary/manager, Michael Turner. Turner is that rare bird who is capable of combining administrative skill with human understanding, and he immediately recognized in Illingworth the all-round talents needed to reconstitute a Leicestershire team which had begun to slide back downhill after the emigration to Australia of another expatriate, Tony Lock, who had come from Surrey to lead Leicester with unexpected flair and resolve. Turner convinced his trusting committee to guarantee Illingworth the one thing he'd craved for but never got at Yorkshire, freedom to choose his players and to lead them in his own way. No one should underestimate the 'eminence grise' role of Turner in bringing about the Indian summer of Illingworth's latter years. Certainly the man himself has often spoken of his positive relationship with Leicestershire's chief executive. Open praise of this sort from Illingworth is as rare as a full toss on a turning wicket!

Talking cricket with Ray Illingworth, OBE, is an endless experience. On this occasion we met in the physiotherapy room at Grace Road, Leicester, at the beginning of the 1977 season. As always, the captain was first at the ground and – wholly in character – he had the first and last word!

ILLINGWORTH: If I were to break down tomorrow and never play again, there's very little I'd look back on with regret. In the twenty-seven years I've been in the game I've been

The fruits of victory

involved in teams that have won eight County championships, taken all three limited-over competitions, gained sixty-six England caps, thirty-six of them as captain, and I'm the last English captain ever to win the Ashes in Australia ... and there are only three of us! No, looking back I've few complaints, although it didn't always seem so rosy.

WALKER: Let's look first at the blacker moments. I suppose your leaving Yorkshire under an acrimonious cloud must have been the worst?

ILLINGWORTH: No, I think losing the captaincy of England to Mike Denness in the middle of the Test match against the

West Indies at Lords in 1973 was. I know that I'd made a few hackles rise because when I was captain I usually got what I wanted, particularly in regard to the players in the team. There are, or were, some people in high places who didn't like relaxing their power. I think to be an England captain who survives you've either got to be successful or else be a bit of a creep and a social climber. The only reason I lasted as long as I did was because the England team's results meant they couldn't drop me. As soon as we had a real stinker – like the first innings against the 'Windies' at Lords – they knifed me. Look what then happened. It's only in the last series out in India in 1976/7 that we again began to have any shape about our team, and then right out of the blue the captain abandons ship! I can understand the lure of the money, but Tony Greig is anyway the highest-paid cricketer in the world, making I guess around £40,000 a year. How much does he want? But to get back to your question. Of course leaving Yorkshire was a wrench, but I don't think it really cut me as deeply as it did Brian Close. After all, I wasn't captain when I left, he was; but we shared several criticisms of the club. Like the system they had when we were playing, that the team was picked by thirteen area representatives of the committee; the captain never got a look in! When I asked for a fixed contract period to give me some stability, their refusal was the final straw. They didn't appreciate that you can't treat people as if Lord Hawke was still in charge! Yorkshire acted as if the players were just another part of the office furniture.

WALKER: What was it about Leicestershire that attracted you? Was it just the offer of the captaincy? Surely you could have got this at a couple of other counties with greater traditions and certainly better prospects?

ILLINGWORTH: It was an easy decision actually. There were a lot of things to be considered, not least that it wasn't all that far south from Pudsey, where I lived. But the thing that tipped the scales was the man in charge at Grace Road, Mike Turner. We go together like two bits of bread and butter. He's a far-sighted, straight-talking secretary who has the complete faith and backing of his committee. They in turn give him his head to gather together the right side and to run the administration of Leicestershire. He in turn leaves the tactics and team selection to me. Mike would make a terrific MCC tour manager, because he knows exactly his role and where he can take pressure off the captain. As a former player himself he understands the mental processes that cricketers go through, particularly during an out-of-form period, and he's young enough not to be too remote. When I agreed to join the club I insisted on having the final say in all matters that affect Leicestershire on the field. He agreed unconditionally. At the start of each season we have a policy meeting with the committee, then it's all up to me. I'm the sole selector. The buck stops with me. t's a good system, even though I've no objection in principle to small selection committees providing they see enough cricket. I joined the club initially on a twelve-month contract to see if we suited each other. That was nine years ago, so we must do.

WALKER: Your name has been mooted as a possible English cricket 'supremo'. When you eventually stop playing, would you fancy this sort of managerial role?

ILLINGWORTH: Yes. But I'd need a few years of uninterrupted planning guaranteed first. If I'd had my way five years ago I'd have gone straight to either Boycott or Greig as my successor as England captain, missing out Tony Lewis and Mike Denness, and I'd certainly have played youngsters like Gower, Athey, Botham a lot earlier. At Yorkshire we believed in throwing kids in at the deep end, head first. If they came up for air and survived, you had a player in the making and quickly. We nurse cricketers too much in this country. I also believe in discipline, and this must come from the captain and manager, not the administration. For instance, at Leicestershire I insist on the old-fashioned virtues of tidy dress, on and off the field. Ties are usually worn on arrival at the ground, although I'm not too fussy about this providing the casual clothes are clean and smart. We wear our blazers at lunch – unless it's very hot or there are special circumstances.

Having these sorts of small but important rules helps to weld people together, gives them a corporate interest and common purpose out on the field of play. Looking around the present first-class scene there are a few too many transistor-listening, aimlessly wandering young men in the game. If I were overall chief I'd make every one of the seventeen first-class county staffs know the sort of attitude I would be looking for. If they don't want to conform, that's their decision, but I know what I want and I think my achievements with Leicestershire and England bear out that I've been right more times than not.

WALKER: Captaincy, leadership, have always been your forte. Have you found it an easy role?

ILLINGWORTH: Yes. I actually captained Yorkshire for several seasons before I left. I had a good relationship with Brian Close and we used to work out the tactics together. I've got a very simple set of rules about captaincy. Whenever and whatever decision I make I do it in the total belief that it's best for the side. Once I've made it, right or wrong, then I expect the absolute support of the team. Sometimes a bad decision can be rectified if the other ten give a hundred per cent. Just as I'm the one who sets the course, I'm also the one who'll take the stick if it goes wrong. In every side there are senior players whose counsel one values, and naturally I'll listen to their thoughts and advice. But in the end the final decision's mine and that's the only way to run a team. Like selection, you can't do it properly by committee.

WALKER: Who then have influenced you and made you the man and the cricketer you are?

ILLINGWORTH: The first proper coach one meets as a boy is nearly always the one who matters. I was lucky in that at the time I joined Yorkshire in the early Fifties, Arthur Mitchell was in charge. He was the straightest, most honest man I ever met. He hardly ever praised a youngster, so that a 'well played' from him was like getting a knighthood! Many years later I heard that someone had once chided Arthur for being so severely critical of the younger members of the staff at that time, in particular me. Arthur had replied: 'You've got to be hard on them. If that lad Illingworth doesn't play for England it'll be my fault.' I don't think today's players are prepared to listen to constructive criticism like they used to at Yorkshire in those days. When I left the county in 1968 Bill Bowes, another big influence in my life, said to Doug Padgett: 'Raymond'll captain England in eighteen months.' It's this sort of foresight, recognition and guidance that is invaluable to an up-and-coming player. Good coaches don't have to always encourage and say what a marvellous player you are but you can sense what they expect of you and so you try to live up to their high standards. This is especially so in Yorkshire and I hope we're on the way towards creating the same sort of atmosphere here in Leicestershire. I've been accused of having a chip on my shoulder, particularly about the way Yorkshire treated me. In this respect, yes, I have. Do you know that when I left the county after giving them sixteen years' loyal service I received the letter from the secretary saying they were not going to offer me a contract which began: 'Dear ~~Ray~~ Illingworth'. They couldn't even bring themselves either to call me by my first name or use a fresh bit of paper! That's one thing that really gets up my nose ... people who call me by my surname. They always appear to be talking down to me.

But to get back to players who've helped or influenced me. Well, my first Test captain, Peter May, will always hold a special place. After we'd won the Ashes in 1971 he dropped me a line of congratulation saying that he'd taken a far better team to Australia in the 1960s and lost the series 4-1: well done. That meant a lot.

WALKER: Moving into the present, what impact, or legacy if you like, do you think you have left to the current bunch of England players?

ILLINGWORTH: Well, I brought up most of the now senior members of the side. I think what I did for people like Alan Knott, John Snow, Derek Underwood, Geoff Boycott, Tony Greig and Dennis Amiss was to treat them as men. I tried to take away from them the feeling of fear when they first came into international cricket. Fear of being dropped, fear of personal failure and also fear of the administrators. I always stuck my neck out for them and the players knew that. I remember one of Tony Greig's first Test matches. It was at Old Trafford, Manchester. We were having a meal in the hotel restaurant and the bill came to £2.75 a head. Our meal allowance then was £2 and Donald Carr, who was in charge, said we would have to pay the difference. Tony put his hand in his pocket but I said no we were playing for England, we had eaten the meal we required and we didn't intend paying the 75p excess. After a long debate and several consultations with other officials, I won my point. I know this impressed Tony. It's a small story with a big message which showed the future England captain that in the end it's the players who count and the players who should be looked after.

WALKER: Since the war, excepting Bradman you've played against all the finest players in the world both here in the United Kingdom and in their own countries. Who do you particularly rate?

ILLINGWORTH: Oh, Len Hutton for sure. Such a beautiful style, the real essence of cricket for me. He was such a good player on a bad wicket, with a superb judgement of length and a technique which allowed him to change the whole motion of his stroke at the very last second. I believe that after watching Greg Chappell and Gary Cosier get five wickets apiece in England's innings during the Prudential Cup match at Edgbaston in 1977 he said – and Len's a man of few words: 'I'm sixty-one, but I think I could have taken a few runs off those two lads, you know.' I believe him! He was head and shoulders above any English player of my time. Peter May was the best killer of a bowler I've seen. If you bowled averagely well at Peter he'd murder you, unlike Colin Cowdrey. Even on a good wicket I always reckoned to be able to contain Colin because if you bowled a decent length and line he never really took the offensive. For sheer courage I can't think of anyone to match Ted Dexter in 1959/60. The way he took on Hall, Griffiths, Rorke and the rest around that period was like a throwback to the days of the old bare-knuckle fighters! He's the hardest driver of a ball I've ever played against. It's one of cricket's tragedies that he lost interest in the game so young, he should still be playing now. Not a captain's backside, mind you, too full of strange theories, and his mind on the day's race card, but in his day what a player!

In technical terms Geoff Boycott's the best batsman in the world today. His problem is his own insecurity. He's never trusted people and I think this facet of his personality comes out in his batting style. I'd always fancy my chance bowling on a turning wicket against a great player like Barry Richards, who always gives you a chance. Boycott in similar circumstances would quite possibly get a hundred.

Sobers? The best of all time, he's certainly the finest batter I've ever bowled against and the sheer range and improvisational qualities of his stroke play made it quite impossible to set a field to him. One could have nightmares thinking of the West Indian batting line-up in the 1960s with Sobers coming in at number 6 or 7! I always admired Ray Lindwall for his control, Fred Trueman for his strength – he could come on at ten to six at the end of a long hard day and bowl as fast then as he had at the start – and what a glorious action! A real picture model for youngsters. Then Brian Statham, who had so much heart. Day-in-day-out he'd turn in performances of real class, often bowling uphill into the wind. And of course, Wes Hall. In that great Test match at Lords in 1963 he not only bowled thirty-odd overs in the day but he'd started at 11.30 with two freshly bleeding blisters the size of pennies on his feet. A great trier. Of the current players you've got to look at a couple of other West Indians, Clive Lloyd and Viv Richards. They don't come much better.

WALKER: You've just had a testimonial season with Leicestershire. How much longer can you, or do you, want to go on playing?

ILLINGWORTH: If you could issue me with a new back, another two or three years. I get a fair amount of pain in one of my lower discs. The one-day cricket's the hardest, the John Player League especially so. Batting where I do I often find myself trying to run like Jesse Owens to keep up with people like Roger Tolchard and Brian Davison. No-can-do. The tempo of one-day cricket also puts an incredible strain on captains; I don't think many people appreciate this. I'm not a great lover of the purely defensive field placings which one has to adopt because containment is more important than getting wickets, so my enjoyment of this sort of cricket is less. Mind you, limited-over cricket keeps me young, or at least I like to think it's helped me stay in the game as long as I have. When I have to go, it'll be with great sorrow, because despite the various hands, I'd never change the way the cards have been dealt to me. Mike Turner wants me to stay with Leicestershire in some capacity and there's also possibly the England job we've talked about. I'd enjoy that because, unlike a lot of players, I'm an avid watcher of the game. Even now I'm still picking up little things that I never knew went on.

PS During the winter of 1977/8 Illingworth announced that at the end of the 1978 season he would be rejoining his old county, Yorkshire, in the newly created post of team manager. He envisaged no problem or clash of personality with the club captain, Geoff Boycott. It's no secret, however, that his decision came as a surprise and a shock to Leicestershire who were making plans to retain his services in a similar capacity after his playing days were over.

Not classic but so effective

Richards: a man alone

Barry Richards

'The world's best' is a subjective judgement on the part of the writer, and so when I propose the motion that Barry Richards of Natal, Hampshire and South Africa is the finest opening batsman in the world today and has been for the best part of the last decade, I cannot substantiate this with international figures.

Ever since his country's expulsion from the world arena in 1970, Richards has had to plead his case on the lesser provincial stages of England and back in his native Currie Cup competition. At thirty-two he's in his prime, yet for all his enormous ability and past record he remains a complex, shadowy and sometimes misunderstood cricketer, certainly the most unrepentant mercenary amongst the many overseas stars who have dominated the professional game in England since the latter part of the 1960s. There is scarcely a batting record that he hasn't held at one time or another, and he is one of the few men to score more than 300 runs in a single day's batting. This came during the 1970/71 season in Australia, where Richards had gone in the English off-season to play for South Australia. He reached 356 in all, including 325 on the opening day of the match at Perth against a Western Australia attack that included Dennis Lillee. His innings lasted a mere 330 minutes on the first day and included 137 between the lunch and tea intervals!

To put this innings in perspective, since the war, besides Richards, only Jack Robertson of Middlesex and England has made over 300 in a day! Like all articles of true artistic worth, it's impossible to put a price on Richards' skill, though he himself did just that during his season with South Australia, when he organized sponsorship for himself at a dollar a run for the season! No other player in contemporary world cricket, not even his namesake Viv Richards the West Indian, makes batting look easier.

I first came into contact with the South African when he, together with another Natalian, Mike Procter, came over to join the Gloucestershire second eleven for a season's experience in 1965. He was then just twenty but I remember he and Procter playing at the old Cardiff Arms Park against Glamorgan in a friendly match. Richards only made a dozen or so runs but the class in both these young South Africans was obvious. Dennis Compton had mentioned to me that he'd been in South Africa the previous winter and had seen, in his opinion, the best young batsman since the war. That boy was Barry Richards. At this early stage of their development, the bowling skills of Mike Procter remained dormant, and it was his close friend from Durban, Barry Richards, who looked the better prospect. But after one game in Gloucester's first team against the 1965 South Africans, where he made 59, the streak that has often perplexed people who don't understand the makeup of the man took Richards away from Gloucestershire, who had given him his initial break, into the arms of Hampshire after a 'Dutch auction' with Sussex for his services.

Even as recently as the late 1960s it was almost unheard of for a cricketer wishing to change counties to throw in his hand to the highest bidder. The concept of loyalty to one master, one's first county, was almost sacrosanct, a factor which helped to keep wages low. With the Test and County Cricket Board registration laws then making any move extremely difficult and initially unprofitable to both the recipient county and the individual player, a soccer-type transfer system was just not possible. If anyone has helped loosen the hold on a player's individual right to play where he chooses, on his own terms, then Barry Richards must be considered the principal instigator. Even when he was in his early twenties and relatively unproven at the highest level, his potential was such that he could virtually name his own terms to his prospective employers. He was certainly the first professional county cricketer to break through the £2,000-per season barrier in the days when an established Test player like Fred Trueman would just about reach that figure providing he played in all five Test matches during the English summer.

To this day Richards remains an unrepentant mercenary, offering for hire his talent to be able to bat better than anyone else alive. When the mood takes him, other individuals and the team ride to success in the wake of his brilliance. Gordon Greenidge, his West Indian opening partner at Hampshire, freely admits the enormous debt he owes to the example and encouragement of Richards. Since the South African joined Hampshire in 1968, they have won the County Championship in 1973, the John Player League in 1975 and the Fenner Trophy in 1975, 1976 and 1977.

Yet in spite of his impressive list of individual contributions, Barry Richards remains a curiously uncertain man. Technically there are purists who would say that because he finds the demands of batting so minimal he tends sometimes to allow his footwork to become lazy and thus occasionally has to stretch for the ball a long way from his body. My experience against him as an opposing bowler is that if this be the case he does it merely to set himself fresh technical problems in manoeuvring the ball through the field. His stance at the wicket is comfortable, erect and deceptively casual. True, the feet do not travel vast distances either forward or back, but they move enough to get Richards into line with the ball and, more importantly, to keep him perfectly in balance as it arrives.

I've bowled many overs of medium pace and slow left-hand spin at Barry Richards with all six balls pitching somewhere near a length around about the off stump. Occasionally, very occasionally I might get away with a maiden over but it would depend on a high level of agility from the fieldsmen and a measure of indulgence from Richards himself! More often, an over would cost a dozen or more runs with the boundaries coming from such divergent areas as third man, long off and deep mid-wicket. He's the complete batsman, with the skill and inner confidence to seemingly predetermine, before the ball's on its way, exactly where he's going to hit it. I've seen him do precisely this against medium-pace and even genuine fast bowlers. If he lacks something, and this has been a constant factor throughout his first-class career, it's the mean, killer instinct that was part of the batting makeup of people like Bradman, Hanif Mohammed and Len Hutton. Richards is easily satisfied.

Once, after getting a hundred against Glamorgan in a Sunday League match at Southampton during which he literally toyed with our attack as if it were merely providing him with some casual net practice, he threw his wicket away. The match was being televised. Richards the entertainer had provided the licence payer with his Sunday's entertainment and there was no need for him to belabour the point.

But having said this, Richards, like all top-class performers, needs an occasion, like television, to raise his own game. A bad batting wicket is another challenge he revels in. Almost alone of the overseas stars who have joined the county circuit, Richards is a consistent heavy scorer on indifferent pitches.

Despite his easygoing exterior, a natural facet of a character formed in the warm outdoor life of South Africa, Barry Richards is very much a loner. Acquaintances he has by the hundreds, true and meaningful friendships are as few and as scattered as thunderstorms in the Karroo desert. Batting is a lonely pastime. Nearly all the greatest players have been selfish men, men who hog the strike when there are easy runs about, men who keep away from a dangerous bowler until either he tires or else the batsman's confidence improves to the state where he feels equal to the task, and men who play for themselves looking for a not-out innings which will

Everything right

improve their average even though the game's situation cries out for chances to be taken in search of quick runs. Richards is guilty of perhaps only the first charge, but such is his skill and awesome runmaking speed that there are few who would call this a fault.

And of course there is the manner in which the runs are

made. A full pickup – even against the fastest bowlers – the smooth, unhurried movement into position and the graceful swing of the bat which sends the ball powering away to the boundary with as much apparent effort as you or I would take to push back a well-oiled sliding door.

Richards' first-class record in Britain and abroad is well documented. It is not the purpose of this piece to spell it out in detail or analyse his many memorable innings. I'm far more interested in the man himself, particularly as I shared a similar kind of upbringing in that rightly criticized but often misunderstood county, South Africa. As a loner it could not have been in Barry Richards' nature to involve himself in the struggle for sporting equality in that country; yet he was one of the original activators in the struggle towards complete racial integration in his country's cricket.

Regrettably it seems now that the world will only have a chance to see just how good he is against international fast-bowling opposition – men like Holding, Roberts, Daniel, Croft, Lillee, and the rest – in the Kerry Packer artificial circus atmosphere in Australia.

It's common knowledge inside the game that everyone likes to be able to say that he's bowled out Barry Richards. At Southampton the level of combat between Richards and Test match bowlers in touring sides is precious little short of the real thing, and his record here stands comparison with the best.

Profiles and articles about Barry Richards understandably concentrate on his prowess on the field, but while I would be amongst the first in the queue for tickets for one of his command performances, it's the man underneath the shock of unruly fair hair who fascinates me more. There are so many contradictions as yet unanswered: by himself too I suspect. A man who plays for pay with a singlemindedness unusual in cricket, which despite its professional structure remains curiously and in many ways charmingly amateur in its execution. A man who is upset by failure yet who outwardly seems indifferent, even bored, in the daily chore of the playing the game. A personality whose broad streak of fatalism is completely and absolutely repudiated by the way he expresses himself at the crease.

We've talked on many occasions. What follows is a distillation of our conversations down the years, either out in the middle, in a county club bar after a game or during a Sunday League teatime interview on BBC 2 lasting seventeen minutes. I think they reveal a side of Barry Richards which perhaps even he would not immediately recognize.

WALKER: I can't remember having played against someone who makes batting look so easy – or for that matter one who gives the impression of believing it is. Is cricket really such a straightforward game for you?

RICHARDS: Hell, no. Of course it's a façade. Every batsman has his own particular mannerisms. Mine is to appear offhand and a little disinterested. But underneath I'm as nervous as every other cricketer, particularly in the moments just before going out to bat. That's the worst time for me, as it is for all specialist batsmen. Once I'm out in the middle, things drop into place, but the waiting is hell. I know that there are some people who say I'm bigheaded, arrogant if you like, when I'm at the crease. Far from it, I can tell you, and I think you'll find that the opposition out on the field would agree with me on this. I'm not really what I would consider, or would deep down like to be, a confident cricketer. Some players have come up to me and said: 'I wish I could play like you.' Frankly I often wish I were someone else. There's an enormous amount of pressure on me, particularly over the last seven years when I've had a fair amount of success at the game. Early on I used to enjoy the publicity and the reflected glory that went with it. But now? Well, I've had enough. With Hampshire I've been lucky enough to win both the County Championship and the John Player League and the only major regret I have is that I haven't had a chance to prove myself in the Test arena. Mind you, the same could be said of a lot of very fine South African cricketers. In the early 1970s I think we had a side that could have beaten the world, and that from a cricketing population of under 50,000! But now I've had a skinful and can honestly say that I never again want to be right in the centre of the spotlight. In any case, with my temperament I think I'd be a better player in a more relaxed atmosphere with less pressure.

WALKER: I've heard it said that you don't really enjoy playing cricket – that you find the day-to-day county circuit irksome and that sometimes you don't bother to try simply because on the day you can't work up enough enthusiasm for batting. Is this true?

RICHARDS: You're right, it can be difficult. But having said that, I can't recall ever having consciously given my wicket away. Looking back I can remember occasions when I wasn't fussed one way or the other if I got out or not. There was a time in 1971 when I'd had enough. I'd played too much cricket, two summers in England with a hard winter in Australia in between. During this period I frankly didn't enjoy my cricket much. I'm a 'mood' player and I've found that I need regular extended periods away from the game to retain my interest. I think in the UK we play far too much cricket. I'm not the sort of player who can give one hundred per cent all the time, and people who come and watch me, or employ me for that matter, just have to accept this fact about me. Mind you, I'm aware – and it would be hypocritical to say anything otherwise – that I'm often the one people have come to see bat. And immediately we're back to that pressure bit. I'm just incapable of concentrating on every ball of the day, seven days a week, which is what is expected of me. 1968 is a good example of what I mean. I got 22 scores of 50 and over and yet only five hundreds that season.

WALKER: I can't altogether go along with your pessimistic assessment of your approach and application to the game. Nobody could play so positively or successfully and not be a cricketer of exceptional inner motivation.

RICHARDS: Objectively, I suppose you're right. I've never really gone through a bad patch in my life. I'm not playing particularly well at the moment but I'm still getting runs, so there must be something inside me which wills me on to success – even though I think I'm a pessimist at heart!

WALKER: The word 'great' is bandied around almost without thought these days but surely you must consider, if only by looking backwards at your record, that you're a great batsman in the true sense of the word. Does this label give you any pleasure?

RICHARDS: It really depends on who calls me or writes about me being a great player. I get more pleasure out of overhearing say a county player call me this than reading it in all the national newspapers put together. I value the respect of the ordinary English pro more than any other section of the cricketing community. It also depends, too, on how one defines greatness. By style, ability, application or adaptability? It matters who's asking the question. For me it's the ability to score consistently fast. Ask yourself how many batsmen you would put into this category. I can only think of two – Gary Sobers and Graeme Pollock. Five or six others come near. I certainly don't. I've never seen Graeme struggle after reaching 50. I might be better, or sounder, up to the half-century, but then Graeme accelerates away, leaving me standing. To me the art of batting is not hitting the ball hard, but rather being able to place it wide of fielders. Someone like Gary or Graeme can bludgeon the ball two feet wide of cover and it's four runs. Not me. I'm very weak in the wrists and I need the pace of a bowler or the wicket to help me guide the ball where I want to. Then all the best players I've watched move back and across with their rear leg as their first movement. I try this too.

There's another attribute as well. A great batsman can hit the ball well in the air. I don't – I mainly keep it along the ground. Do you know, Peter, in that innings of 356 in Perth, I only hit one six, but there were 48 fours!

As for bowlers, I can think of several greats. For me, John Snow in his prime was the best quickie I've ever played against, but for sheer speed I can't imagine anything quicker than Thompson and Holding. When you bat against REAL pace the ball literally passes you like an express train ... it makes a sort of 'whoosh' sound. But although it needs a lot of power and coordinated strength to bowl fast, quick bowlers are a delicate lot in that some days when everything clicks they're like lightning, or other days, hardly above fast-medium. I would say that the most consistent quick bowler playing in English county cricket these days is Andy Roberts, the West Indian who plays for Hampshire. Mind you, I see him every day of the week, but Andy is almost always consistently fast through the air. Thomson gets the most bounce from the wicket of any bowler I've played against – it must be something to do with his slingshot type of action – and of course before he had that knee injury my old pal Mike Procter could make a batsman jump around a bit.

Spinners? Underwood, Chandrasekhar and Bedi on a turner are all a threat, though being primarily an offside player, I don't really mind facing the ball which spins away from me, whatever the speed or bounce.

WALKER: I've known you now for the best part of twelve years, in fact from round about the time you joined Gloucestershire as a teenager along with Mike Procter. After a season there your name was linked with Sussex before Hampshire came along with a better offer. Although you've stayed with them, there have been the odd rumblings of your holding out for more pay and even threatening to give up cricket altogether or move to another county unless Hampshire came up with a better offer. Things have been quiet on this front for a couple of years now but there have been some rather unkind things said about your commercial attitude to the game and that you're inclined to give your loyalty to the club with the biggest purse.

RICHARDS: Not so. I won't ever deny that I want the best financial return for my skill. What's immoral about that? I happen to be a professional cricketer, that's my training, that's my talent, and it's the only way at present that I can make myself a decent living. I'll not deny that the 'dollar a run' incentive I played for out in Australia made me a better player. Whereas before I'd been a sort of airy-fairy type of batsman with success coming pretty easily, that extra incentive made me a much more determined character and certainly more singleminded about making big scores. In fact, looking back, I played that season in Aussie with the same sort of application I'd had around about 1968 when I was trying to establish myself in England. Since then I've made a better than average living out of cricket. But remember, it's others who approach me with offers, I haven't ever gone around peddling my wares like some kind of tout. If someone wants to hire me for my cricket abilities, whether it be as a player or a coach or as an after-dinner speaker, then I don't think it's unreasonable for them to expect to pay the top rate. I'm not comparing myself with a 'professional' man in the same sense as a lawyer or accountant, but assessing cricketers' values is a bit like looking for a motorcar to suit your needs and pocket. You get what you pay for.

Incidentally, I don't consider myself to be avaricious. In my early days I was paid well under the then going rate for people like Kanhai, Gibbs, Engineer and Procter. All I attempted to do in the period when I was negotiating my salary with Hampshire was to bring myself up to their level. I didn't think then that this was unreasonable and I haven't changed my mind now. I know I've said, or been quoted as saying, some pretty selfish things. I don't deny many of them and looking back I'd be the first to admit that I brought a lot of justifiable criticism and trouble upon myself. I wanted too much too soon I think, and probably I expressed this rashly at the time. If I had my time over again I'd certainly be more tactful. I think at thirty-two I can now handle both life and success much better than before – but behind my earlier attitude I think basically lies the fact that I'm a pessimist by nature. I've a dread of insecurity – my father had a tough time when I was in my early teens – redundancy and all that goes with it – and the spectre of poverty and the avoidance of it used to haunt me continually. Not so much now that I'm established in the game, but it could crop up in a couple of years' time, who knows?

WALKER: Why?

RICHARDS: Well, I've bad ankles, the right worse than the left. I wouldn't be surprised if my playing days were over by the time I'm thirty-five. Also I want to try to obtain a few agencies for sports goods in South Africa and work on developing them out there. Inevitably this would mean less cricket, and I'd give up the seven-days-a-week grind in England right away. Also I'm a great believer in getting out when I'm at the top.

In the next four or five years I want to create enough opportunities both in and out of cricket so that I'll be able to stop when everyone still remembers my good days. I don't suppose many batsmen score a higher percentage of 50s than I do, so I feel I can still contribute for a couple of years yet. I wish I'd been a better bowler because time certainly drags in the field.

WALKER: You were one of the group of leading South African cricketers who organized and took part in that token walk-off at Newlands in 1971. It was a demonstration that showed that white players in the Republic were concerned about racial discrimination in team selection out there. Are you by nature a liberal?

RICHARDS: By South African standards, certainly. But then liberalism is a dirty word out there. I'm certainly not martyr material or by nature a demonstrator or believer in causes. But my experiences over here, playing with cricketers from all backgrounds, colours and creeds, have convinced me, something which isolation out in South Africa would never have, that we all deserve a fair chance. For instance, when I go back to Durban and coach for the Kingsmead Mynahs Club, I'll coach anyone – Indians, Cape Coloureds, Chinamen – just so long as they're interested in cricket.

Incidentally, this is one question I resent from pressmen. It's the interview which always looks for an angle rather than my opinion about cricket. Papers send journalists out to talk to me who know nothing about the game. I'm prepared to talk to them about cricket and cricketers and leave it at that. I want to be remembered, if at all, by my skill as a player and if possible as a responsible, likeable person who has grown out of a turbulent adolescence into a worthwhile member of society. Cricket has given me the opportunity to prove the first part – continue giving me the chance and I know I can do the rest.

Cartwright – perpetual motion

Tom Cartwright

Every so often cricket throws up a performer whose talent arouses a sense of awe amongst his fellow players. Such a man is Tommy Cartwright, capped a mere five times for England in the 1960s, but a bowler of such enormous skill and application that his name is used throughout the cricketing world whenever the subject of conversation turns to the definition of the word 'professional'.

I first met Tommy in the late 1950s when he was on the Warwickshire staff. Then he was a front-line batsman good enough to score 2000 runs in one season, with a top score of 210. But as is so often the case, as one part of his game blossomed, the other branch, bowling, languished. He'd always been considered a useful medium-pace net bowler, but when three Warwickshire seam bowlers suddenly retired within a couple of years of one another he seized the opportunity with typical tenacity.

The medium-pacer is the lynch pin of English county cricket, a fact which mystifies people overseas, where such kind are regarded as cannon fodder for batsmen and in terms of importance about as useful as cold water at a banquet. Abroad it is either sheer pace or artful spin that count, but on the more yielding English pitches, where the ball gains enough purchase to alter direction if pitched on the seam and will also swing in the heavier, water-charged atmosphere, bowlers like Cartwright, Lever, Hendrick and Botham are guests of honour. Yet medium-pace bowling, with its lack of visual aggression or artful flight, finds few sympathizers either in the press box or from supporters on the boundary edge. But, as the Americans neatly put it, on the receiving end it's a different ball game!

For one thing, when bowling on a helpful pitch, a class performer like Cartwright not only makes the ball deviate in the air with late swing either way but also causes it to alter direction after landing. When all this happens inside the space of half a second from the time the ball leaves his hand until it arrives at the other end, the problems of combating it are colossal. Genuine fast bowlers are usually pretty straight from hand to bat. Spin bowlers, because of the parabola of the ball, do give you a split second in which to change either your stroke or your mind ... or bòth. But the medium-pacer literally gives you nothing. He's the meanest man in cricket. Because of his reduced speed compared to opening bowlers, his control over length and direction must be far more accurate, particularly if the pitch is unhelpful and the atmospheric conditions not conducive to swinging the ball in the air.

It's in this way that Cartwright in his prime was unique in contemporary English cricket. An assassin on a wicket which gives him the slightest encouragement, he's capable, even at the age of forty-two, of sending down over after over of minutely directed just-short-of-a-length bowling which eventually makes even a batting Job commit hara-kiri! No one else in the game combines skill and application to such a degree.

Cartwright has suffered numerous injuries in recent years, particularly to his right shoulder, where a series of operations, each in theory serious enough to terminate his career, turned out to be successful repair jobs on surely the most overworked ligaments in any professional sportsman's body. Surprisingly for a man with so much mileage under his belt, Tom Cartwright is something of a hypochondriac, and his past injuries, while admittedly serious, have tended to keep him out of the game for long periods.

He's also a man of deep personal convictions, with the

same obstinate qualities in his conversation that characterize his bowling. This has resulted in ruptures of a different kind. First with Warwickshire, when he left on a matter of principle in 1969. Then towards the end of the 1976 season his contract was terminated with Somerset where he'd gone via a year's sabbatical coaching at Millfield Public School after leaving Edgbaston. An illustrious career seemed over until a former Warwickshire colleague, Ossie Wheatley, now chairman of his adopted county Glamorgan, thought he still had much to offer.

In a sense he has come home to roost in Wales, for in a first-class career which spans twenty-five years he's taken a shoal of wickets against Glamorgan and his wife Joan, a keen cricket supporter, first met him during a game at St Helens, Swansea. His role with the Welsh club in what must surely, even by his own resilient standards, be the tail end of his career, has been spelled out. It's not so very different from what he's done so well in the past. To add substance and steel to the county's attack and to instil in the Welsh county's several promising young players a sense of pride of performance and a dedication to the grind of mastering the basic skills of a complex and often heartbreaking game.

When I come to picture him in the twilight of my life, it's the run-up and delivery action I shall remember as much as anything that subsequently happened down at the receiving end. The seven-pace run-up begins with a small dip of the slicked-down, centre-parted black hair. The jaunty, slightly bucking stride brings him easily to the crease and the swing into the delivery position is a coaching manual's illustrated dream. Up goes the left arm high, leading shoulder well round, front leg braced, the head rock still and the eyes looking over the shoulder down the wicket at the blade of grass the ball is intended for – at least, one could swear that he has a solitary piece in his sights! The delivery itself is high and loose, but well controlled, with the right arm classically brushing the ear as it sends the grenade on its way.

Between his ears is the bowling 'Brain of Britain'. Cartwright has an encyclopedic memory of batsmen and their habits. The grunt of effort that accompanies each release of the ball has a variable pitch depending on what type of delivery he's bowled; and the range of that is considerable too! Originally he only bowled inswingers to a heavily packed legside field, relying on the slant of the ball to a right-handed batsman to hit the inside edge or catch him lbw. But he soon altered the groove of his action and broadened his horizons to include not only the ball which went the other way in the air towards the slips but also variations of movement either way off the pitch. In his next season it was possible to read from his action which way the ball was going to swing in the air (no one, not even the bowler, can nominate with certainty what's going to happen after it has pitched). But inside another twelve months, Cartwright had so honed and refined his new-found skill that the subtle changes in his body and wrist position at release were almost undetectable. From now on no one was safe, and for the next fifteen years Cartwright, together with Derek Shackleton of Hampshire, who operated in similar style, was consistently amongst the heaviest wicket-takers in the game, Tommy's biggest crop being in 1967, when he took 147 first-class wickets in all.

Cricket has unquestionably been the dominating force in his life, yet unlike so many other accomplished sportsmen, Tom is both intelligent and objective enough to analyse not only his opponents' strengths and weaknesses but also his own. It's with this in mind that we sat in a basement corner in the Swansea pavilion and talked.

WALKER: Batting as often as I did against you, Tommy, I recall how impressed I always was by what I believe are your two main qualities – your obvious control over where the ball is going and the unrelenting strain you place upon a batsman by bowling at a particular weakness of his. How much of this do you work out beforehand?

CARTWRIGHT: Oh, I can remember back years and years how I got such and such a player out. Especially if he is a

Length and line

big-name batter. Before each season I look down our fixture list, which grounds we are playing at, and even at this early stage I begin to think about how to bowl at the key batsmen in each county. I don't believe any bowler worth his salt would give you any different answer.

Knowing your opponent in cricket is just as important as in boxing, and rather like boxing there is a softening-up process which a bowler like myself, who lacks real pace, has to inflict on a batsman before attempting to drive home the knockout blow. I always bowl with a pattern in mind. By that I mean I size up batsman 'A' and decide on a certain combination of deliveries which will set him up for the wicket-taking ball.

I never run up expecting every ball to get a wicket. I think in two or three-over permutations – like a series of outswingers delivered from wide of the crease getting the batsman accustomed to moving his feet into one position. Then I'll try another outswinger, this time from close to the stumps fired across the batsman. Unless he is a very fine player, there's a good chance that his feet will go into the position from which he played the earlier deliveries but that the wider angle of the ball swinging away towards the slips will drag him after it. It could hit the edge, or if the ball comes back from off the seam, 'go through the gate' between bat and pad and bowl him. And if it hits him on the pad, I might get an lbw decision. This is how I always bowl. I really concentrate on putting a planned series of deliveries together rather each bowling each ball with everything in it.

WALKER: Very few batsmen have ever managed to give you any real 'stick', regardless of the wicket, but is there anything at all which can disrupt this almost metronomic quality in your bowling?

CARTWRIGHT: Slack fielding. When I'm trying to get a batsman committed to play, say, down the wrong line by, if you like, showing him a few red herrings like I mentioned earlier, and then someone misfields, giving him a single and allowing him to get away from the strike, I find this very annoying. It's rather like having the black ball over a pocket in snooker.

You've only got to sink it to win the game, but somebody wets the tip of your cue and the stroke misfires.

It's after such an incident that I'm most likely to bowl a bad ball. It's spoilt my concentration. When I bowled 77 and then 62 overs in separate innings in the Test series against Australia in 1964, the concentration required was colossal. But the challenge of doing well in county cricket is just as intense, and I have been at it so long now it comes automatically to me at this stage of my career.

WALKER: Much is talked about how precise and constant a batsman's concentration has to be. I don't believe, and I am sure you'll agree, that enough is made of the similar effort required by bowlers. As far as I'm concerned, bowling 40 accurate overs absorbs as much mental energy as scoring a hundred.

CARTWRIGHT: Of course you're right. Easily the most important aspect of bowling is the ability to concentrate totally on what one is trying to do. A genuine quick bowler or fingerspinner can get away with the odd really loose ball, but at medium pace, a slight wandering away from length and line almost certainly means four runs. It's a hell of a strain to bowl accurately for a long spell. I nearly always bowl with a short square leg, and I know above all else that his physical safety depends on my accuracy. This is an added burden for me, and after a long day in the field I often come off feeling as limp as a rag through this accumulated anxiety.

WALKER: If this is the case, how on earth do you manage to turn in such consistently high performances virtually every day of the summer?

CARTWRIGHT: I believe that successful bowlers like myself, for whom accuracy is a key weapon, are able to recover physically much quicker than other bowlers. I'm thinking of men from the past like Derek Shackleton and Don Shepherd. I rarely go to bed before midnight but my constitution is such that inside twelve hours I've rebuilt myself if you like. A tired bowler just puts the ball on a spot as opposed to bowling it with real snap.

We are playing so much cricket these days, travelling vast overnight distances to do so, that I'm sure that throughout the country a great number of the younger quicker bowlers who might be basically fitter than me are tired 'inside' by the middle of a season. This means a slacker concentration and a corresponding loss of control and tautness, if you know what I mean.

WALKER: Yes, I do. Your action has been described as economic but technically perfect. It should be filmed in slow motion and used in an MCC coaching scheme. Have you always found the mechanical side of bowling, if I can call it that, easy?

CARTWRIGHT: Oh, no. Accuracy I've always had to work at. I know I've a good basic action and I think I learned how to bowl really straight early on in my county career in the late 1950s. We had covered wickets then, and at my pace I had to bowl accurately to survive. Until I did my National Service I could only bowl awayswingers, but after two years in the army I must have grown, because my action changed slightly and I could only bowl inswingers; I'd lost the outswinger completely.

But after being demobbed, I played at Dudley in the Warwickshire first eleven and suddenly I bowled one awayswinger, completely out of the blue. Luckily, I'm aware of what the different parts of my body are doing during my action and I was able to remember how it had happened and so repeated the delivery.

WALKER: If you were advising someone on the basic principles of bowling, forgetting for the moment the intricacies of swing and movement off the pitch, what would you advise them to do?

CARTWRIGHT: Keep their head still throughout the cartwheel of the arm-swing. Wrist position, height of arm and release, angle of hand, grip and placement of feet are all relatively unimportant. All the great bowlers – and batsmen for that matter – are very much like top-class golfers. Their heads are very still throughout the swing. So it is with bowling. To anyone who is not bowling straight – and this is the easiest part of bowling – it's probably because your head is wobbling as you release the ball.

Remember Shackleton? Never a hair out of place even after 40 overs! Once your head is still, try not to cut across the ball with your fingers at the moment of release. Swing comes from one's body action, and particularly the position of the wrist. The key to all movement of the ball is what you do with your wrist. Above the shoulder it's the only thing I alter each ball. On a wicket which gives some help to bowlers of my type, I reckon to be able to bowl the ball that comes back into the wickets after pitching from outside the off stump at will by pushing the inside part of my wrist through first as I let the ball go while retaining the seam in a vertical position.

There is one little theory I have why some cricket balls swing more than others. It may be just quirk, but I believe a ball with a lot of gold lettering stamped on the cover will not swing as much as a plain one! It will only do so after 15-20 overs have been bowled when the lettering has been worn smooth by constant rubbing on the bowler's flannels. It might sound odd to you, but I believe this anyway.

WALKER: Have you ever had a day when everything seems to desert you – where you lose your accuracy, swing and concentration? I ask you because this happens to many bowlers I know.

CARTWRIGHT: No, I can't say that's ever happened to me. At least, not all those things at once. It sometimes takes me five or six overs to get my action right, however.

If I start bowling and everything doesn't click immediately, I've got eight or nine standard checks I run on my action – rather like a pilot doing a systems test at the end of a runway before taking off. But principally I'm concerned with making sure that my arm is high at the point of delivery and work down the list from there. I can usually do something with the ball either in the air or off the wicket in this country, but swing doesn't get many good players out, in spite of what happened in Massie's Test match at Lord's. That was a rarity.

On good wickets I use angle and width variations at the crease delivered at an identical target area as my main wicket-taking ploy. I always try to keep the pressure on batsmen by denying them runs, because if you persevere long enough and bowl with attacking fields, you can feel the tension in him mounting. Any batsman will eventually go a long way towards making a fatal mistake if you create this sort of atmosphere.

Few bowlers these days, and one-day cricket has accelerated this I'm afraid, are prepared to work on a batsman in this way. Mind you, it's got to be happening at both ends to be really successful. I used to like bowling in Test matches with Fred Titmus at the other end. He approached bowling in exactly the same way as I do.

WALKER: You've mentioned how much you analyse opponents and remember how you dismissed them in previous encounters. Think of a couple of examples just to round things off.

CARTWRIGHT: Well, I used to get Geoff Boycott out regularly because he misjudged length. But he is much better now than he used to be on that score. Then Tom Graveney always used to be a candidate for a bat-pad catch early on if I could bring one back at him. Both Boycott and Graveney were quite easy to bowl at because they rarely attempted to play the ball in anything other than an orthodox way. Sir Garfield Sobers was a hell of a difficult man to contain before he came to play full-time in this country. There really was a batting genius. You could bowl six identical balls at him and he'd belt you to six different parts of the field. But once he'd played a fair amount of county cricket for Nottinghamshire it became much easier, though not always possible to keep him in check. I'm sure this is because a lot of our game is played in the dressing rooms and many reputations are built up there as we discuss various players. Gary must have been influenced in the way he played me by what the other Notts boys said, because I know they rate me highly through having several good matches against them.

Roy Marshall, the former West Indian Hampshire opening batsman. Well, he was a destroyer of any bowling that was in the least bit wide of the stumps. You had to bowl very, very straight at Roy to keep him quiet, and after a couple of early tries I never bowled an outswinger to him in the last ten years of his career. He used to murder them!

The art of bowling is the developed ability to read batsmen, to propel the ball with accuracy into the target area over long periods, to be as mean as Scrooge about giving away runs and never to release the pressure on a batsman, however well set.

Fredericks the Bold

Roy Fredericks

Roy Fredericks is not a big man – he is only five feet four inches tall – but as an opening batsman of international stature the Guyanese left-hander ranks with the highest. He's been in and around the top-flight scene since 1967, when he scored 127 and 115 against Barbados in the Shell Shield. The next year he won a place in the West Indian party to Australia, where he averaged 33.87 in the series. Since then his position in the national side has never been seriously challenged.

His three-year stay in English county cricket was always exciting, frequently brilliant, often stormy and eventually ended in acrimony. He was first seen in the United Kingdom in 1969, when he became the only member of that West Indian team which included Sobers, Lloyd and Butcher, to top 1000 runs on the short tour.

Like so many Caribbean cricketers, his ability to play the game lifted him clear of a bleak financial future. But for cricket he would probably have spent his days as an insignificant filing clerk in Georgetown, Guyana, where he was born.

The advantage of playing in the close proximity of local luminaries like Clive Lloyd, Rohan Kanhai, Basil Butcher, Joe Solomon and Clyde Walcott, who was then the Guyanese coach in the early stages of Fredericks' development, helped to mould a technique and an attitude which enabled him to overcome the handicap of his lack of inches. Quick on his feet, a wristy cutter of deadly certainty, the perfection of his timing sends the ball flying away to the boundary with an incredible speed considering his body weight is under ten stone. The advantage of batting on the true-bounce, even-paced wickets of Guyana gave him the early confidence to play his strokes with total freedom, so that by the time he arrived on a three-year contract for his first professional engagement with Glamorgan in 1971, he was pretty nearly at his peak.

His introduction to English county cricket could hardly have been more dramatic. Fredericks had been signed as a replacement for Bryan Davis, the Trinidadian batsman who had played a substantial part in the Welsh county's winning the Championship in 1969, the year Prince Charles was invested as Prince of Wales. Davis had sought and found a better livelihood outside the game back in his home town of Port of Spain. Jeff Stollmeyer, the former West Indian Test captain, suggested Fredericks as a suitable replacement, and he duly arrived at the April pre-season nets comparatively unknown in this country despite his tour of 1969. He was selected to play in the first county match of the season early in May 1971. The venue, Trent Bridge, Nottingham. He made 145 in the second innings, took five wickets in the match with his left-hand chinamen and googlies, and was awarded his county cap at the end of the three days!

It was an eventful season for the diminutive left-hander. In his first home game for Glamorgan against Worcestershire, fast bowler and fellow West Indian Vanburn Holder made a ball rear off a length and broke Fredericks' right forearm. He missed the next six weeks' cricket but on his return still reached 1000 runs for the season at a club average topping 45.90 runs per innings. Reviewing the season, *Wisden* wrote: 'There were some who believed that Fredericks' adventurous approach was an embarrassment. He was a law unto himself, but let it also be admitted that he brought a breezier and fresher gust of gaiety to the cricket grounds of South Wales. His two innings at Swansea against Northamptonshire and Yorkshire will remain in the memory of cricket cameos for all time if only for the joyous abandon of his batting.'

It was this quality above all others that endeared and yet infuriated members, paying spectators and his county colleagues, for during his three-year spell on the seven-day-a-week United Kingdom circuit he never managed to add a measure of consistency to his repertoire. Even in Test matches, he still has two sides to his cricketing nature. The brilliant cavalier, capable of being out first ball by accepting the challenge of the short-pitched ball and hooking it for 6 or straight down the throat of a fielder at deep fine leg; or alternatively destroying an attack completely as he did in the fourth Test match at Headingley in 1976, when he scored a breathtaking hundred in the first innings. Then there was the annihilation of Lillee and Thompson at Perth in 1976, when his century not only helped the West Indies to win the game but has passed into history as one of the six most sustained exhibitions of scientific hitting ever recorded.

The other side is the ultra-cautious sheet anchor, the mantle he unconsciously inherited from Conrad Hunte. His 150 in the second Test against England in the 1973 season, which took eight and a half hours, is a classic example of this Jekyll and Hyde aspect of his character. But it must not be forgotten that on this occasion he rescued his team from a potentially lost situation with a masterly exhibition of self-control, a feat that won him the Prudential-Wisden award.

Like so many cricketers from the Caribbean, Fredericks is a quick learner, explaining no doubt why it is that cricketers from that part of the world seem to reach maturity so much earlier than those in the United Kingdom. His experience on English wickets paid off when on a difficult Port of Spain pitch in the second Test against New Zealand in 1972 he made 69 and 31; two innings which he regards as technically the best he's ever played. I remember Freddie telling me at the beginning of the summer of 1972: 'The experience I gained playing on English county wickets helped me tremendously. I never really really watched the ball until I joined Glamorgan. Playing all my cricket on flat West Indian and

Australian wickets had made me technically a little slack. You don't have to concentrate so hard at home. Once you're in and have got the pace of the pitch and the bounce of the ball, only fatigue or carelessness should get you out. In England it's so different. You can get a ball bowled at you when you're 40 and set, which is totally unplayable! Playing in English conditions made me a lot more selfish. By that I mean that once I get over the initial few overs and survive, then I try to make the most of my time at the crease and not throw it away as I used to.'

Yet inside eighteen months of his telling me this, he'd been thrown away by Glamorgan, sacked. The arguments then put forward for this extraordinary decision, taken when the club was near the bottom of all the competitions and left rudderless by the retirement of Don Shepherd and a number of other senior players, still does not make sense five years after the event. It was alleged that the little man did not try when playing for his adopted county. Yet the crowds loved him and in his three years with Glamorgan he consistently either topped the batting averages or was never out of the first three. There was also the laudable statement that the club wanted to encourage local talent. They then promptly went out and made a disastrous signing of a wayward Barbadian fast bowler, Gregory Armstrong!

There is no doubt that Roy Fredericks was and remains a moody player. The West Indian personality is by nature a happy-go-lucky one, ill equipped to tackle disaster, and Roy is certainly archetypal in this respect. He is ultra-sensitive to criticism, loath to take advice that isn't self-originated, and from the county's point of view he did prove a law unto himself by flouting pre-arranged tactics.

But his virtues overall far outweighed his faults, and he injected into the Glamorgan team a sense of fun and enjoyment from playing the game that proved infectious. Asked how he felt just before going out to bat, the invariable answer would be: 'I tink I'm agoin' to pelt some lash at de ball, man.' And lash it far and wide he often did.

'6 or out?'

Since leaving the county Roy has made a secure future for himself back in Guyana, but I like to recall the time I first talked to him in May 1971 in the days when he was fresh to the United Kingdom. Fresh in the sense that he was emerging from the all-embracing clasp of a touring team to prove himself as a solo artist in the most critical arena of cricket, the County Championship. We chatted in the buffet of the train as we journeyed back to Wales after his first week in professional cricket.

FREDERICKS: I suppose I'm pretty typical of most post-war West Indian cricketers. Ever since I made my debut for Guyana, against Trinidad in 1964, I've thought about playing professional cricket, but of course until the county registration laws were relaxed it just wasn't financially worthwhile to spend two years qualifying in a second team. I've four brothers and a sister, but surprisingly I'm the only one in the family with any interest in cricket.
WALKER: You're established as a West Indian International opener, but just how much experience have you had?
FREDERICKS: Well, I went to Australia in 1968-69 and played in every game but one and then toured England in the West Indian side which came here for the latter part of that season. I played in eighteen games, more than any other player. After we went back home I became the national coach to Guyana, which meant teaching at schools all over the country. And of course I've played in the Shell Shield competitions over the past seven years and in four of the Tests in the series against India which has just finished.
WALKER: This is particularly interesting to me because India are due to visit us in the middle of the summer. Although the West Indies lost the series to them, India rarely do well in this country. Is their team going to do any better than the previous ones?
FREDERICKS: In spite of us losing the series, I don't think the Indians will win a Test match over here. Their batting is only fair – Gavaskar and Sardesai scored 776 and 624 runs, and

the next best was 224, so they were terribly dependent upon these two. Both are strong 'bottom-hand' players, with great strength on the legside, but as always they're susceptible to real pace. On the only quick wicket we played them on, in Barbados, Vanburn Holder scythed through them and so England, with Snow, Ward and Shuttleworth, will have a big advantage here. If they're going to do well, then it will be because their three world-class slow bowlers, the offspinners Venkataraghavan and Prasanna, and the left-hander Bedi, are allowed to pin down the English batsmen. They're very accurate, and Venkat in particular spins the ball a lot. But they didn't endear themselves to our spectators because if things were going against them they would drop down to 14 overs per hour – Bedi sometimes took six minutes to bowl an over!

WALKER: We read here criticism of Gary Sobers as captain, especially after you lost the second Test in Port of Spain and there was a call for the selectors to appoint Joey Carew as captain in his place. Has Sobers the confidence of the team?

FREDERICKS: Oh, there's no question about this. To the players Sobers is the captain. And as far as we are concerned it's very difficult to imagine playing under anyone else. I'm sure Gary is in the captain's saddle for a long time to come.

WALKER: When Bryan Davis left us at the end of last season we obviously had to look around for a replacement. I'll be honest, Roy, the first we as Glamorgan players knew of your coming was an announcement in the press just five weeks ago. How did the offer from the county reach you?

FREDERICKS: Well, Jeff Stollmeyer had been asked by the Glamorgan committee to see if any established West Indian players were interested in joining the county. I know they had approached a Guyanese team-mate of mine, Alvin Kallicharan, but Warwickshire stepped in first there. Jeff wasn't aware of my interest, but when he did hear that I wanted to try my hand he immediately contacted me, wired Glamorgan, and within ten days I'd agreed terms and was a Glamorgan player! I will say one thing, though. Before the deal was settled I'd spoken to Bryan Davis in Trinidad, Rohan Kanhai and Clive Lloyd, and they all said that Glamorgan were one of the best teams in the country and I couldn't go and play with a better bunch of lads.

WALKER: I remember from my own experiences of two tours to the West Indies that people out there are very aware of English county scores and the players involved. How highly thought of is county cricket in the Caribbean?

FREDERICKS: We recognize it as the best cricket in the world and players like Gary, Rohan, Clive, Lance, and the others are always stressing this point at home. I suppose this is why so many of my countrymen want to come here – it really means something back home to succeed in the UK.

WALKER: You've signed a three-year contract. Will you stay in the game in this country for this period only or have you got longer-term aspirations?

FREDERICKS: Well, Peter, I now regard myself as a professional cricketer. To us West Indians that means playing cricket or coaching cricket all the year round, if possible.

WALKER: Yes, but surely this will mean you'll rapidly become stale and in consequence not play anywhere near your true ability – even Sobers and Kanhai have suffered from this, and I'm sure that last season's wear and tear on Lancashire's Clive Lloyd affected his performances against India where he only scored 295 runs in the series at an average of 29.

FREDERICKS: Yes, I appreciate this is possible – in fact I feel rather stale myself at the moment. But you people in England just don't realize what cricket means to us – it's one way of gaining people's respect, recognition, and eventually, one hopes, a good job. I'd like to play every day of the year. To me the hardest part of this coming season could well be trying to get used to all these lettuce lunches – Gary told me he's estimated he's eaten eight tons of lettuce since he started playing cricket in this country!

WALKER: How confident, then, are you about making an impact in this your first venture into county cricket? Do you think it will be easier than, say, succeeding in the Shell Shield competition in the Caribbean?

FREDERICKS: Oh, no. Of course I'm apprehensive. I know that batting in England, or should I say Wales, is going to be far tougher than at home because the wickets vary so much. We always reckon that if you succeed in the UK you can succeed anywhere. I'm anxious, too, because I'm playing in strange conditions, a long way from home, with players I don't know, and I'm very aware that everyone in the county is expecting me to do as well as Bryan Davis did.

Although I don't bowl much at home, I'm hoping to get in a few spells of some left-handed wrist spin, because so few English batsmen seem to read this type of bowling. It's been a happy start so far. I felt I played pretty well at Chelmsford in the first Sunday League game of the season; the club have fixed my wife and me up in a very comfortable furnished flat in Swansea overlooking the bay; and from my first meeting with the Glamorgan lads I think I'm going to be very happy in Wales. Out in the West Indies we feel that of all the people in Great Britain we have more in common with the Welsh than any other race. Even the way we speak is vaguely similar.

If things go my way I'd like to spend the next ten years – or if you like the remainder of my active cricketing life – playing here in Britain. In fact, if I can get a clerical job here I'd like to stay for the winter as well; but of course this will depend on the West Indian selectors; if they want me for the coming series at home against New Zealand, then I'll go back. But right now my heart, my home, and my ambitions are here in Britain, and if I can help to win the County Championship for Glamorgan again, then it will be the greatest thing which has happened to me since I started playing cricket. After all, this is where the game began, and this is where all players have to eventually test and prove themselves.

Greg Chappell

The other day I was looking at a newspaper photograph of Greg Chappell, Australia's former captain and leading batsman. Alongside it, by way of comparison, was one of Jack Hobbs, scorer of over 61,000 first-class runs including 197 centuries. Below the neck the likeness was quite remarkable. I never saw Hobbs play in the flesh but I have been very close to Chappell, particularly during his two-year stint with Somerset in 1968 and 1969.

Comparison between the English master batsman and twenty-nine-year-old South Australian-born Chappell is by no means odious. Both justify the appellation of 'art' when applied to batting, both employ a simple but classical method, and each projects a deceptive illusion of having plenty of time to stroke away even the fastest bowlers.

The Chappell pedigree too would no doubt have pleased the late Sir Jack. Victor Richardson, who led Australia with much distinction in the 1930s, is the grandfather of Greg and his brother Ian, the former Australian captain.

Without wishing to sound patronizing, I believe Greg Chappell to be one of the more charming cricketers to have come from his part of the world in the last decade. Cricketing abilities aside, he thankfully lacks the aggressive 'Strine' aspects of his brother Ian's character, an attitude which bred a close-knit Mafia-type bond amongst the team which toured the United Kingdom in 1972, making social exchanges between the touring party and their hosts often extremely difficult. In a manners sense there were frankly some deplorable incidents during that trip, which were tactfully not reported, but following Greg's accession to the throne there was a gradual return to the old traditions and spirit. This is not to say that the recent Australian captain is a 'soft touch'. He is, and has always been, fiercely patriotic and on the field a typically uncompromising Aussie. But I believe his short stay in the first-class game in the United Kingdom when he was at an impressionable age helped to smooth the hard edge of irrational anti-Pommie resentment which his brother never ever lost.

Despite one or two troughs, Greg's cricketing abilities have never been questioned. He made his first-class debut for South Australia when he was twenty, scoring 53 and 62 against Victoria. Like so many overseas players, he is an exceptional athlete in a number of ball games, while in his first love, cricket, besides batting so brilliantly he also bowls either medium pace or legspinners and even has kept wicket when required! So when he signed for Somerset he came over as a young, inexperienced all-rounder who could do a bit of everything.

There is nothing so salutary as repeated failure in the lonely vocation of professional cricket, and for the large part of his first year in 1968 he knew more despair than elation. His home-grown technique, though fundamentally sound, was inadequate for the slower, more devious English pitches, and mid-off and mid-on had a field day as he regularly holed out there from mishit drives. But with characteristic tenacity he stuck to it, so that in 1969 he blossomed to become Somerset's leading batsman, scoring 1330 runs at an average of 30.22. He also took 45 wickets into the bargain and held 21 catches.

In parallel to his efforts on the field, he was developing as a person too. Some of his ways, like going barefoot in the dressing rooms and pavilions and his penchant for outrageous clothing by English standards, raised an eyebrow or two at Taunton, Bath and Weston, but these personal idiosyncrasies apart, he was recognized as basically a 'good guy', and the disappointment was acute when he decided to call it a day at the end of his second season and return permanently to Australia. Colin Atkinson, now headmaster at Millfield School but then a member of the selection committee, was convinced that the club were losing a potential world-beater who was on the point of realizing his latent talent. Still, despite Somerset's entreaties, Chappell, showing a hereditary side of his personality, refused to change his mind and went home initially to a job with the Coca Cola organization and inevitably a place in the Australian Test side.

Greg was among the last of the band of modern Australian cricketers who entered service with English counties. He was followed at Somerset for a short spell by Kerry O'Keefe but the post-war group who had spread themselves among the seventeen counties – Jack Pettiford of Kent, Bruce Dooland and Alan Walker of Nottinghamshire, Jack Manning, Jock Livingstone and George Tribe of Northamptonshire, John McMahon of Surrey and Somerset, Colin McCool and Bill Alley of the same county, Ken Grieves of Lancashire, Jack Walsh and Graham McKenzie of Leicestershire – had or were soon to disappear. In recent years only Bruce Francis, briefly with Essex, and Alan Connolly, whose spell with Middlesex was even shorter, have bothered to come to this country to develop or expand their talents. Nowadays it is cricket-hungry and financially less well-off West Indians who dominate the overseas contingent who 'play for pay' on the county circuit.

But although Chappell's stay in the UK was short, there is now a great deal more English method in his batting style than home-grown Australian. This was graphically illustrated during the 1977 tour of England, where he alone of the party had the technical equipment necessary for consistency of performance in a summer where pitches so often helped bowlers of all types. The comparison between his figures and those of the erratic Doug Walters, on his fourth tour of the United Kingdom but still playing like a beginner, illustrates what I mean; Chappell scored 1182 runs, averaging 59.10, Walters 663 runs at an average of 26.52.

On their most recent visit to the United Kingdom the new breed of Australian batsmen by and large found it a terrible uphill battle. Those with the power of absorption and the humility to learn went back to Australia better players who will surely in years to come return to take revenge. But in this trough in their cricketing history, Greg Chappell stands on a pinnacle.

He was in a particularly difficult position, for in the early part of the tour a premature leak of the Kerry Packer 'cricket circus' plan put an enormous amount of extra pressure on the Australian captain, one of the original signatories to the pirate scheme. Relations with tour manager Len Maddocks inevitably became strained because Maddocks, a former Test wicketkeeper and an influential member of the Australian Board with which Packer is in a state of open warfare, found himself in an impossible position – that of managing a side nearly all of whom from the captain down had mutinied! The analogy between Maddocks and Captain Bligh is inescapable.

If Barry Richards was the first of modern cricket's mercenaries then Greg Chappell will surely be looked upon by historians as Commander in Chief. Although Tony Greig's defection and subversive activities quite naturally received more publicity in this country, Greg Chappell, backed behind the scenes by big brother Ian, is the one around whom the current crop of young Australians ranged themselves.

Let there be no question about it, the lure has been gold. The waffle about the games between Australia and the Rest of the World producing a higher standard of cricket is pure hyperbole. If it is about anything at all, Test cricket is all about national rivalries, and Chappell and his band have chosen to wave two fingers at over a hundred years of Anglo-Australian conflict on the cricket field. His was a hard-headed and well considered move. It remains to be seen whether the insurrectionists have won the day or if the traditionalists will regain the upper hand.

Knowing the man, I suspect that Greg's assessment of the situation was that he would have played no more than another two years' international cricket anyway before outside pressures from family and business forced him into retirement from this level. This was reduced to a premature giving up of the captaincy which he announced at the end of the fourth Test at Headingley where England regained the Ashes.

Chappell – smooth as silk

It is difficult particularly in defeat to blame him for now seeking the best financial return from a game which has given to and received so much from him.

So much for the broader issues of the Packer affair. For the moment my subject is Chappell the cricketer and the man. What follows is a distillation of several conversations I had with the Australian captain during his two most recent visits to the

. . . and brutal with it!

United Kingdom – in 1972 when he topped the touring averages, 1260 runs at 70.00, and again in the summer of 1977 when we sat on the roof of the Gloucestershire county ground soon after he had returned from making a masterly 102.

WALKER: You look in pretty good nick at the moment, Greg.
CHAPPELL: Yes, I am, it certainly makes sitting out here in the

sun a lot more pleasant. Like all sports, the afterglow if you've had a successful day is nice and warm. But playing so much cricket as we do, one comes to realize that it's here today, gone tomorrow. You can't succeed every day of the week, so it's important to keep a sense of perspective about it all.

WALKER: That's a surprisingly humble point of view coming from an Australian! As a nation I wouldn't say you're over-renowned for your sense of modesty.

CHAPPELL: Oh, I don't know about that. I've met a goodly number of one-eyed bigots and certainly far more two-faced people on the fringe of cricket in this country! Australians believe they are born winners. Success at sport means a lot to the average Australian, and it carries a lot more social prestige than it does in the UK. To do well at games can often mean – as it has to both Ian and me – a useful leg-up towards getting a good job outside the game. Mind you, the climate makes it a lot easier to get involved in outdoor sports.

But I'm sure my having played here before and knowing most of the county players is a bonus for my own confidence. It's much easier to do well in an atmosphere one knows and has succeeded in, so in a way, whatever position I might have achieved in cricket, or will gain in the future, brings me back to the debt I owe to my two-year county stint with Somerset, for it equipped me to survive in international cricket.

I think my attitude, or philosophy if you like, was largely formulated during my stay with Somerset, but that two-year stint was also long enough for me. You play too much cricket in this country. To succeed at the highest level you need plenty of breaks in between Tests – at least I do, which is why I sometimes copied my brother Ian's idea of handing over the captaincy to one of the other senior players during county matches. In part, the sheer volume of cricket in this country was a major reason why I didn't accept another contract with Somerset. Playing day in day out I found that bad habits quietly but quickly crept into my game, and because you play so much here they tended to become grafted onto my technique by sheer repetition. One game just blurred into the next ... Taunton

Wednesday, Worcester Saturday, Hove Sunday, Leeds Wednesday, back to Taunton, and so on. It's not so bad if you're in a touring team because you can take matches off and get away from the game. You can't do this as a contract professional.

But having knocked the structure of cricket in the United Kingdom let me also put the record straight about its importance in my own development. 1968 and '69 were easily the most formative years of my cricketing life. It was pure chance that brought me to England. I wanted to play county cricket but no one county seemed particularly interested. Hardly surprising – I was eighteen years of age and my only credentials were that I had played Grade cricket in Adelaide and was Ian Chappell's kid brother! Then I got 150 in a Sheffield Shield game at Perth which was seen by a Somerset vice-president living out there. At that time the county were negotiating with John Inverarity, but he was picked for the 1968 tour of England. So because the season was only just around the corner, in desperation Somerset signed me on their vice-president's recommendation. When I came to this country I was a legbreak bowler. The single-wicket competition which Bass-Charrington used to sponsor turned me into a seamer. But I didn't mind because in Aussie nearly everyone is a bit of an all-rounder, otherwise if you're a specialist batsman you can go three weeks between innings in club matches. Broadening this, I think this is why Australians are such good competitors. We HAVE to succeed each time we play, because our opportunities are limited. Being involved in the county cricket scene, the will to succeed is reduced, because there's always another game tomorrow. When I came over I was fully prepared to honour the whole three years of the contract. However, towards the end of my second season, for the reasons I've already mentioned, plus the offer of the job with Coca Cola, who said they'd give me all the time off I wanted to play cricket in Australia, I asked Somerset to release me. They were very good about it and I've remained in touch and kept on friendly terms with them ever since.

In a cricketing sense, playing in the UK did two important

things to my game. It made me play straight through the pitch of the ball instead of slightly across it, as I had been doing on the better wickets of Australia, and secondly, it taught me how to concentrate for long periods.

WALKER: I know that concentration is the one requirement of batting you put higher than any other. I'd like to hear your definition of it and how you go about fixing your mind so precisely for long periods.

CHAPPELL: I think concentration begins long before you even get to the ground. I make a point of not trying to anticipate what's going to happen. Back in Adelaide in the early 1970s I did a fair bit of coaching with people like Gary Sobers, Lance Gibbs and Barry Richards. They all instilled into me the importance of analysing my own game – where my strengths lay and, more important, where I was vulnerable, and why. Barry has undoubtedly been the biggest influence on my career. He's such a good coach. During this period we used to spend a lot of time together away from the game as well. He's the one who I've tried to model myself on, if you like – not stylistically, but mentally, and the way he approaches the problems of batting.

I like to sit by myself before I go out to bat. Anyone will tell you it's very difficult to get into the right frame of mind if there's a lot of noise or chatter going on in the background. Batting and concentration are two things which improve if you form good habits. For instance, I try to play very, very straight when I first go in. Basically I've always been a front foot player. My stay with Somerset didn't change me in any way, but batting on slow, often unpredictable-bounce English pitches did force me to watch the ball a lot longer than back home. There, once you've got over the first twenty minutes or so, the bowler doesn't get you out, you commit batting suicide! Over here I find even when I've got 30 or 40 on the board I have to concentrate just as hard as if I were playing my opening overs. My stint in England certainly tightened up my powers of concentration because of this.

When I go to the wicket I talk to myself a lot. I mentioned about playing straight. By that I aim to hit every ball I'm forced to play back in an arc between mid-off and mid-on. I keep saying to myself something repetitious like: 'Watch the ball, watch the ball.' I do this from the time the bowler begins his run up. Come to think of it, I talk to myself throughout my stay at the crease. Once I stop doing this I know my concentration is beginning to slip and then I'm really in trouble. That's what I mean by having good habits. If after a couple of overs I notice that I'm not talking and preparing myself, then I know exactly what's happening to me mentally.

WALKER: Do you talk out loud much while you're in the middle?

CHAPPELL: A fair bit, yes. But I don't talk to the fieldsmen – they're there to get me out! I certainly exchange the time of day with the umpires. It's a form of relaxation really. You can't keep yourself wound up into a tight introspective ball all through a long innings. A couple of words with a second party gives me just the break I need before returning to the job. Incidentally, I haven't found captaining a difficult or heavy burden. It certainly hasn't affected my international performances since I took over from Ian. But there is a lot of extra work off the field, particularly on tour. You're on duty twenty-four hours a day. If the Kerry Packer offer hadn't come along I think I'd have done this year and one more as captain and then called it a day.

WALKER: What can you tell me about the Packer deal and why you and so many world-class players have accepted his terms?

CHAPPELL: I'm sure we'd all say the same thing. The money was too good to turn down. It's a straight business deal so far as I and I suspect the rest of the lads are concerned. Kerry Packer came to us to buy our particular skills. There's absolutely no difference in this to any other normal business deal. Having said this, it was still a difficult decision for me to make. Initially I thought it was too complicated to work, but despite what's now happened I believe it could have been feasible to work out a short series like Packer's and still accommodate it inside existing official plans.

But look at it this way. I was coming towards the end of my

international career. The game's been very good to me and I hope I've done something in return – that's not for me to judge. I accepted the offer because it provides a form of financial security that official Test cricket simply can't. I've found that although I've had a couple of jobs because of my cricket ability, I haven't been able to give them the attention they deserve. For ten years I've travelled the world playing cricket. It's been good to me but it's also meant that I've fallen behind those who work full-time in the commercial world and quite rightly they've forged ahead with promotions of different kinds. Now I want more time with my wife and family. I've spent eighteen of the last twenty-four months away playing cricket. Enough's enough.

Going back to the deal offered by Kerry Packer, everyone made up his own mind – there was no discussion amongst the Aussie Test players. I think our Board is likely to resist what's happened for a while and then a compromise will be reached. Sure, the whole face of Test cricket as we know it will be changed, but I feel no sense of guilt at having helped to bring this about. If there is blame – and I don't accept that – then it must be shared by the administrators. They spurned three earlier offers and so in a way they forced us to go behind their backs. Without Packer's interference I think cricket would have remained in the lower-paid echelons of world sport. Ten years from now the so-called 'circus' could well be part of the normal scene.

On the playing side, cricket is one of the last retreats of traditional sporting values and as a traditionalist at heart I'd be bitterly disappointed if it doesn't remain that way. I like to think my own behaviour and performances have always been in the best interests of the game, and if by this move we can lift cricket up into the 'super sport' bracket, then I'll feel I've done my bit.

WALKER: Was there a turning point in your career? I know a lot of sportsmen can look back and say, it was that particular bit of advice or that particular stroke of luck that changed my life.

CHAPPELL: I wouldn't put it as precisely as that in my case, but certainly there was a time during the 1971 season in Australia when my ability to succeed at the highest level was very much in doubt. I've already said that in my view concentration is the key factor in cricket. Without it you're a non-starter; it doesn't matter how much ability you've got. I was then scoring pretty good twenties and thirties and then getting myself out. I'm reasonably analytical about my own performances and my father was a considerable help at this stage of my career. I've always been aware of press criticism and in 1971 I got pretty sensitive about the way they were writing me off as a mere flash in the pan. But then I realized what they were saying was true. I just didn't seem to have it in me to bat longer than about an hour or so without doing something bloody stupid. Eighty per cent of the time I was getting myself out. I like talking cricket to cricketers and from what they were saying it gradually came home to me that I wasn't really looking at the ball and that my mind was a complete jumble while I was at the crease. It was round about then that I began to talk to myself at the wicket, almost like my conscience was keeping a watching brief over what I was doing. Well, it seemed to work. I got a hundred in the Melbourne Test after being very lucky to get in the side and then 196 not out at Sydney in the next. I've just gone on from there.

WALKER: As a world-class number 3 batsman, you must have particularly vivid memories of facing the world's fastest bowlers.

CHAPPELL: John Snow was the best Test quickie I ever faced. He was so accurate, particularly in the 1971 series when we lost the Ashes to Ray Illingworth's team, and in terms of speed he was really fast. He was a superb competitor, never complained on the field and never apologized! Jeff Thomson's the quickest thing I've ever seen. That slingshot action of his produces the closest thing to a lethal projectile you can get in cricket. And of course Dennis Lillee. A great fast bowler in the all-round sense. And what courage! Three years ago a specialist said he wouldn't walk again without pain, let alone bowl, because of the stresses he'd put on his back during his career. If anything he was an even greater bowler after the diagnosis! That's heart for you. And of course Holding, Roberts and Daniel of the West Indies are all very rapid. Who's the quickest? It depends on the day and how well coordinated they are at that given moment, but Thomson gets my vote as the quickest and most dangerous of them all.

WALKER: What of the future?

CHAPPELL: Well, as I've spent about sixty per cent of my time in the five years since we've been married away from my wife Judy, I think I'd like to get involved in a sport we can play together. Back home we're very pally with Ashley Cooper the former Wimbledon champion and his wife, and we all enjoy a game of tennis. I get bored just sitting around so there'll probably be a bit of golf too. I play off a 'commercial' handicap of 17. It's nearer 15 really! But most of all I'm looking forward to concentrating on my various business interests. I'm involved with an insurance and travel company. Money has always interested me, not just the making of it but the way people use money, and of course I hope to keep in touch with cricket in some way once I've stopped playing.

My family will be my main future interest, particularly my son Stephen, who's two, and Belinda, who was born just as we left for the UK in April 1977. I'm looking forward to instilling in them the love of sport my parents gave to me.

Even the best play across it sometimes

Procter – hired to kill!

Mike Procter

If, as is sometimes suggested, sport and theatre have much in common, then Michael John Procter is cricket's Olivier. After Gloucestershire's victory over Kent in the 1977 Benson and Hedges Cup final he was described as 'the biggest single factor in the reemergence of the county of Grace and Hammond as a power in the land'.

Like all virtuosi, Procter has a sense of occasion, a point graphically illustrated in the semi-final of that same year's Benson and Hedges competition, when singlehanded he wrested the game back from the grasp of Hampshire. His hat-trick which removed Barry Richards, Trevor Jesty and John Rice was seen by millions on television and by a capacity 8000 in the flesh at the county ground, Southampton. On a near-perfect batting wicket, Gloucestershire had made a disappointing 180 in their 55 overs, and against a team which included both Gordon Greenidge and Barry Richards, all seemed lost. Although the explosive punch line in fast bowling is the moment of release, Procter, like Wes Hall and Dennis Lillee, is fully aware that his run-up to that event carries its own additional charge. Coming in at full sail from the end of his 35-yard run-up, the flying, blond-headed Procter is either an exhilarating or a terrifying sight – your attitude depends on whether you're a spectator or batsman!

On this occasion at Southampton, Procter, in mid-over, dramatically switched to bowling around the wicket. The crowd hushed, uncertain and expectant. From near the boundary edge Procter pawed the ground like a Domecq bull awaiting the opening of the corrida gates in Madrid's Plaza Monumental. Then he broke into the stuttering few launching steps that quickly became an onrushing blur of legs and arms.

The analogy between a Spanish fighting bull and the fast bowling of arguably the world's best all-rounder is particularly apposite. Although Procter is above average height, in build he resembles a front row rugby forward ... all neck, shoulders and chest. The breadth of beam across the stern characteristic of most world-class fast bowlers is there too, and the rather stubby legs first smack into the ground as he gathers speed and then stretch out as full momentum is reached – just like a category A fighting bull from Andalusia. The *torero* at the batting crease in his cricketing equivalent of a 'suit of lights' – bat, pads, gloves, box and thigh pad – shares with the matador that moment of true fear as his adversary bears down upon him. And trying to stop a Procter express with a matchstick of a bat must seem like attempting to arrest a bull in full flight with the minute red *muleta*.

At Southampton the parallel became a little uncomfortable as a section of the Gloucestershire supporters – taking as their cue the antics of Lillee fans in Australia – chanted 'kill, kill, kill' in a rising crescendo as the hurtling form of the Gloucestershire captain reached the wicket. Greenidge, one of the finest players of fast bowling in the world, was beaten for sheer pace and had his stumps spreadeagled. End of the over, Hampshire 13 for one. An uneventful six balls of relatively gentle pace from Brian Brain at the other end and it was Procter again; this time versus his lifelong friend and sometime compatriot, Barry Richards. For those present, here was a moment to savour, a rare experience. The world's most gifted all-rounder against unquestionably the finest opening batsman in the game. It was William of Normandy versus Harold of England, Wellington against Napoleon and Dempsey versus Tunney all over again.

Both Richards and Procter knew they were alone on the

stage, totally involved in all the uncertainty of an extemporized drama.

Procter had the first line. A wave of the hand moved a fielder into a closer attacking position, a second shooed three small boys away from the edge of the sightscreen. The principals sized each other up from opposite sides of the stage. Inevitably, Richards had a waiting role, although the final declamation could be his. Far away the figure of Procter gathered itself before launching down his runway like a jumbo jet. Past umpire Spencer flew Procter, travelling it seemed almost at the speed of light, and with that ugly yet wonderfully effective wrong-footed cartwheeling delivery, he spat the ball out like a bullet from the end of a high-velocity rifle. Not only was it fast but the ballistics of seam and shine imparted an inward movement in the air. Richards' blade, the straightest in all Christendom, sought but missed, and to a great hosanna of an appeal he was given out, lbw. Game, set and, as it turned out, match to Procter and Gloucestershire.

To a Hampshire supporter it must have seemed as if Sir Galahad had been unhorsed by a low branch. But although the day and the moment allowed Procter the final curtain, part of cricket's charm is that Richards has had his say in the past and will undoubtedly do so again in the future.

In the bar afterwards the two leading players in the semi-final drama shared, as they always do, a beer at the end of play. 'He's always been a really intelligent bowler,' said Richards. 'He's like Fred Trueman in the way he remembers batsmen's weaknesses and strengths and plays on them. Because he's a helluva good batsman himself, Mike also knows the importance of getting inside the opposing batsman's mind. He knows that by running in a long way and by coming in very fast he sets up all sorts of doubts in his opponent's mind long before he's even let the ball go. Like Fred, he gets a lot of wickets in his run-up! His habit of moving fielders from the end of his run-up is also part of the psychological plan. By shouting his instructions down the wicket he's letting everyone, and in particular the batsman, know that he's working on a plan to get him out.'

The history of sport is littered with the skeletons of promising youngsters who never developed their embryonic potential. This could never be said of Procter, whose prowess even at the age of eleven was remarkable. In that one season he made five centuries including 210 not out against Transvaal schools – a sort of mini Currie Cup match. He was then a wicketkeeper/batsman and in the hothouse atmosphere of Hilton College, Natal, one of South Africa's leading public schools, his all-round sporting gifts quickly blossomed. Barring injury or loss of interest, there was never a doubt that he would one day play for South Africa. In the school cricket first team at fifteen (average age seventeen), number one fly half at rugby for three years, centre forward at hockey, captain of tennis and a member of the squash team!

With his academic background coupled to his sporting abilities, the young school-leaver Mike Procter could have looked forward to a comfortable upper-middle-class life in commerce, but his deep love of cricket first gave him the opportunity and then guided his future in a way that he still finds surprising. A former South African Test captain, Jackie McGlew, arranged for the eighteen-year-old Procter and his Durban friend Barry Richards to spend a summer playing in the Gloucestershire colts and second eleven. McGlew saw in this experience a valuable extension to the practical education of two of South Africa's most promising cricketers which would help to continue South Africa's upward progress in the unofficial world cricket league. But the storm clouds were gathering and with South Africa's exclusion from international cricket in 1970, Procter, Richards, Irvine, Ackerman and a host of other young, talented and highly ambitious performers were left with no shop window to display their wares.

What in 1965 was to have been a summer of acclimatization turned out to be one of indoctrination. Procter had been vice-captain to Richards on a short schoolboy tour of the United Kingdom two years previously and in 1965 Richards and Procter impressed all who saw them. They played against the then touring Springboks and Procter top-scored with 69. But the registration qualifications then existing in English county cricket demanded they had to stay in the United Kingdom for twelve months in order to become eligible to play first-class cricket. Both decided against this and returned home.

But the virus had been implanted during their four-month stay with Gloucestershire, and the next summer they were both back in the United Kingdom – on one occasion taking jobs as dressing-room attendants in order to see the final Oval Test between England the West Indies! When the chance again came to play county cricket, this time they had no hesitation, and deciding that they would have more chance if they split up, Richards eventually joined Hampshire while Procter gratefully dropped anchor in Gloucestershire, the county that had given him his initial break. Since then his feats have been well catalogued, and in 1970 he was elected to cricket's Valhalla as one of *Wisden's* 'Five Cricketers of the Year'.

In 1977 he took over the captaincy of Gloucestershire, heralding a remarkable upswing in the county's performances.

For all this, he remains very much in the engine room of the team, without a shred of the visible conceit which often characterizes a top-class performer. It's because he has retained this sense of perspective despite the reams of praise heaped upon him that Mike Procter remains one of the most engaging cricketers I've met.

WALKER: I seem to recall you saying roughly three years ago that you saw yourself ending your days in Rhodesia. At that time you were the national coach there and were really enthusiastic about the country and the greater sense of freedom you had there compared to South Africa. Then suddenly you moved back to Natal and captained them with great success last season. What caused you to change your mind?

PROCTER: Security. It's as simple a fact as that. I loved and still do love Rhodesia, but with two young children to bring up I gradually came to the conclusion that we couldn't stay there. It made me very sad to leave because I really felt we were achieving something positive in racial harmony terms through cricket. As you know, there aren't many Africans who play the game, but as the national coach to Rhodesia I came into contact with all the Asiatic clubs and schools who needed coaching. Although I wasn't directly concerned with them, I've always been prepared to help or give advice to anyone who asks me. A man's colour or background doesn't come into it. This may sound odd from someone who was born and brought up in South Africa, but then Natal is probably the most liberal province of the Republic. Sure, I was aware of apartheid and what the social rules were, but as a kid at school you just don't think of these things. They're there, so you believe the situation must be normal and correct.

It was only when I came to this country that I began to see things differently. Many people who never leave South Africa automatically accept the idea that the black man *is* inferior. But when I came to England and especially once I made it in the first-class game, rubbing shoulders with great players and real gentlemen like Gary Sobers, Basil d'Oliveira, John Shepherd, Asif Iqbal, Clive Lloyd and the rest, it didn't take very long before I realized that all my inbred attitudes were completely wrong and built on false premises. Now I really have no truck with apartheid. But I still love my country and want to be a citizen of South Africa. That means that whatever my private reservations, I must obey the law of the land. It's a paradoxical situation but one which I must accept or else live elsewhere, and I don't want to do that.

WALKER: Before we leave the subject, I recall that back in 1971 you, Barry Richards, Graeme and Peter Pollock and Denis Lindsay, five of South Africa's leading Test cricketers, organized a symbolic walk-off at Newlands, Cape Town, as your own protest against the Nationalist government's refusal to allow integrated cricket. At that time South Africa had

No need to chase that

only just been banned from international cricket, and as I remember you bowled the first ball of the game for the Rest of South Africa against Transvaal and then you all left the field for ten minutes to issue a statement appealing to the government to allow the Springbok team to be picked solely on merit. In retrospect, do you think that this has had any positive after-effects?

PROCTER: If you'd asked me that question eighteen months ago I'd probably have said no, it had seemed a futile exercise because there had been no immediate government reaction. Now, I'm not so sure, because there is integrated, multiracial club cricket being played in Johannesburg, Natal, and Port Elizabeth, and in other sports too great efforts are being made to remove what we call in South Africa 'petty' apartheid. I know we still haven't got a non-European who is good enough to gain selection for the national cricket team on merit alone, but these are early days, and I've no doubt at all that sometime soon a modern-day equivalent of Basil d'Oliveira will come along and be picked. But who are South Africa going to play against? We are making the effort but it needs two sides to have a game so unless the rest of the world relents then irrespective of what we do, I see no end to the impasse.

But going back to that walk-off in 1971, it's ironic that what we originally conceived as a public plea for moderation was then taken by government sources to be reactionary and subversive. You see, anything that challenges the 'traditional way of life', as the politicians out there love to keep repeating, is regarded as dangerous and extreme! Sure, there have been relaxations all round, we have multiracial athletics meetings now and ex-Wimbledon champion Arthur Ashe is just one negro who has appeared in our tennis tournaments. But it's my belief that until the Springbok rugby team becomes multiracial, the government will never go all the way and throw sport and sports clubs open to all. Rugby is the God in the Republic. The most telling blow ever inflicted on apartheid was the British Lions tour of 1974. A lot of people said that they shouldn't have gone and that the best way to break down the barriers was to ostracize South Africa completely. But, man, they couldn't have been more wrong. Those defeats the 'Boks suffered caused more cracks to appear in the concrete wall of separatism than sixty years of political argy-bargy! Suddenly we weren't invincible any more, and this meant the theory of white rugby supremacy took a body blow.

WALKER: Let's move on to cricketing matters, and in particular your devastating fast bowling. I think if I were a coach and you were a youngster coming to me for advice I'd suggest you concentrated on snooker! Technically you do most things wrong, most significantly by bowling off the wrong foot. This must surely impose a great strain on you physically?

PROCTER: No, not really. It's completely natural to me and I've never felt uncomfortable or suffered an injury because of it. Incidentally, I think it's vitally important to feel comfortable in everything you do in sport. Strain breeds inconsistency. I did have a little knee trouble a few years ago, before the big 'op' I had two years ago. That time I think it was caused because I was carrying too much weight. Being married with two small children soon cured that! When I was a schoolboy at Hilton I kept wicket. Then I played in the national inter-provincial competition called the Nuffield Tournament in 1962/3/4 and towards the end I tried a few offspinners. Just before I finished school, one of our opening bowlers left suddenly, and as I was the only one around, I tried to bowl quick. But it was only after my first season with Gloucestershire that everything clicked. Almost overnight I found I was running faster, bowling faster. The further I ran the faster I seemed to be able to bowl. I need a long run because most of my pace comes from sheer momentum. It would be so much easier and less tiring if I could just take five paces or so, but it's just not possible.

WALKER: You mentioned your big operation. That was to your right knee, and there was a fear at the end of the 1975 season that you would never bowl again.

PROCTER: It actually went back further than that. It all started during a game of touch rugby two days before Rhodesia played a Currie Cup game in 1974. I tore something under the kneecap. Well, I played on with it but it got worse and worse so that in the end during the 1975 English season I had to leave before our programme was completed to fly back for major surgery. What they've done is to remove the cruciate ligaments. To do this they drilled a hole through my kneecap and replaced these ligaments with some taken from the inside of one of my legs in a transplant operation. Then I aggravated it against Lancashire at Old Trafford towards the end of the 1976 season. This happened during the period I was easing my way back into cricket a few months after the operation. I was told by a specialist that I'd never play again, let alone have to give up bowling! Later I was told I could stay in the game but purely as a batsman, and when I came back to this country I did a little gentle training with the Bristol City footballers, which helped enormously. I still get a bit of pain, and psychologically the thought's still there it could go again. Now I suppose it's about ninety per cent right, which isn't bad considering the surgeon reshaped the whole knee. In terms of performance I obviously can't bowl as quick as I used to before the accident: I suppose I'm about a yard slower and now I always bowl well within myself. Experience helps in this, you know. I have improved my line and length a great deal, which means I keep the batsman playing more than before, and of course I occasionally revert to off spinners, so in a way I get more from bowling than I ever did! I would have hated to play as a specialist batsman.

WALKER: You're one of 'Packer's pirates'. Presumably, like the others, it was the money that swayed you, every man having his price?

PROCTER: Yes, it was one of the easiest decisions I've ever had to make. After all, I'm a professional cricketer and when the offer was made to me in London around Easter time it took me less than a couple of minutes to decide to accept. What was also at the back of my mind was the fact that it's a great opportunity for cricketers from my country to get back into the big time. It's my belief that the 'circus' as you call it will last beyond the initial three-year contract period. Kerry Packer strikes me as a man who gets what he wants, and I for one have got faith in him. Besides playing, we fifty cricketers will also do a week's coaching in New South Wales, which must benefit the game in that state. Another good point is that since the news broke just before the first Test in England in 1977, the spotlight has been thrown on to just how badly off the average Test player is. Do you know that they took around £600,000 for the last England/Australia series? The English players got £200 each per Test. That's ridiculous! It should be £1000. Test cricket is what sustains interest in the game, right down to the grass-root level. Where would you get a top-class executive for £40 a day? In business, the managing director doesn't get paid the same as the cleaner. That's the position though in England at the moment.

WALKER: Looking even beyond these present uncertain times, what about your own future? Where do you see yourself fitting in?

PROCTER: Well, captaining Gloucestershire has been a marvellously refreshing experience, and of course winning the Benson and Hedges Cup has done wonders to morale in the club. I'd like to play for at least two to three years after I've had a benefit. I feel really strongly about this because Gloucestershire have been very good to me and I'd like to do as much as I can for them in return. You know we overseas players pick up a lot of stick particularly from certain sections of the press. But I think you'll find that most of us are really attached to the clubs we play for. There's a terrific 'amateur' spirit in the way professional cricket is played in this country.

One criticism I would make, however, and it's against myself as well. Although I think the balance of overseas players to home-grown ones is about right now, with no more than two players not eligible for England in any one team, I think there are too many of us captaining counties. I think the skipper should be an Englishman; it helps to keep the County Championship in perspective. Having said that, I totally disagree with Alec Bedser in his blanket opposition to us being here. I think we overseas players have done a lot for the game, and certainly we've helped to make it the most competitive sort of cricket in the world outside Test matches. If it came to the pinch, I could adapt myself to live in England but if things get too dicey in South Africa (and after Rhodesia who can tell?) then Australia rather appeals to me. I suppose I could get a rep's job out there or do a bit of coaching.

I try to put across the message that cricket is a simple game and most especially it's to be enjoyed. I'm not a great believer in net practice, and success at batting once you've got yourself a sound technique is largely psychological. Personally, I'm perfectly happy to continue as a professional player so long as I get a sense of enjoyment from it. I'm not really an ambitious person and my tastes off the field are simple ones. I love watching TV and reading books by Alistair Maclean and Robert Ruark. I'm not superstitious and I don't think I've got many mannerisms on the field. I haven't got a great historical sense of the game either. I just play as best I can, as often as I can, and I try a hundred per cent each time I go out on the field. There might be a little bit of extra incentive when I'm confronting another international player – I suppose it's part of a fast bowler's pride if you like. I'd love to do the double, but it's not easy these days with so much limited-over cricket. Come to think of it, there's not really a hell of a lot different about me compared to other cricketers.

The third string to the bow – offspinners

Bedi: calm sense of destiny

Bishen Bedi

Within seconds of taking off, Heathrow airport, wrapped in a grey damp February blanket, disappeared below me. The Air India 747 jumbo jet, 'Emperor Akbar', banked steeply and set course for Rome and Bombay. Eleven hours in the air gives one time to reflect on where one's going and the reason why. As the champagne cocktails circulated, so too did my thoughts on what lay ahead.

My decision to go to India to talk to Bishen Bedi had been a sudden one. Yet the idea of including him in this series was at least two years old. He is here of right on two counts. As the best orthodox slow left-hand bowler in contemporary cricket, a position he has held virtually unchallenged throughout the 1970s, and also because the man behind the cunning flight and wicked spin is one of the most fascinating characters in the game today. Naturally enough I have had plenty of time to watch him in action during the English summer while performing for his adopted county Northamptonshire, which at the end of the 1977 season made the baffling decision not to retain his services. His leadership out in Australia in the English winter of 1977/8 , not to mention his own bowling contribution, provided the most damning answer imaginable to the English county. And indeed, besides playing against him for Glamorgan, I've interviewed him during the twenty-minute tea break of a John Player League match televized on BBC 2.

But my instinct told me that to get inside Bishen I needed to see him in action on his own home patch and to talk in an atmosphere that reflected his unusual circumstances as the first and so far only Sikh to captain India. My trip coincided with the start of the fifth and final Test against England in February 1977 in a series where England already held a 3-1 advantage. I had been to the subcontinent once before on a Commonwealth tour of Pakistan in 1968, but India was new territory for me.

My interest in seeing at first hand the fanatical excitement of the crowds and the pressures on international players had been whetted by my county captain Tony Lewis, who had led the MCC team to India in 1972/3. His vivid descriptions of the whole pulsating atmosphere of cricket there had made me determined to see and experience for myself what was obviously a unique set of circumstances, certainly unparalleled in the United Kingdom. With Bedi on the end of the trip, the justification for going was complete.

The 'Taj Mahal' in Bombay is rightly listed among the world's top ten hotels. A huge ornate building on the edge of Bombay's jagged coastline, it stands diagonally opposite the 'Gateway to India' arch erected to welcome King George V and Queen Mary in 1911. A vast rectangular staircase fully seventy feet across surrounds the entrance hall to the 'old' Taj hotel alongside which a new, chromium-plated building carrying the same name but not the 'raj' atmosphere has been built. My arrival coincided with the booking in of the Indian and England teams, who were staying in the same hotel. The atmosphere between the sides was cordial but a little distant, for the allegations of John Lever using Vaseline to polish the ball in the third Test at Madras lingered on. The charge had been made by Bishen Bedi and widely reported in the United Kingdom as an accusation of cheating by Lever, who with five for 59 and two for 18 had largely been responsible for England winning the match by 200 runs and with it the series. While the England players spread themselves around the hotel's pool, the fast bowlers under instruction from Tony Greig to remain in the shade, I went in search of Bedi.

He had not as yet arrived, but his pigeonhole behind the reception desk was jammed full of notes, letters, flowers, bangles and a variety of bric-à-brac good luck charms. To captain India in India puts demands on your time and patience beyond comprehension in the United Kingdom. Although their team had lost the series, a result which meant a substantial loss of face, the fact that India had won the fourth Test at Bangalore with Bedi and Chandrasekhar taking 16 wickets between them meant that the final match at Bombay had taken on the importance of a re-establishing crusade.

The next day was set aside for practice, and I took advantage of an invitation from the tour manager, Ken Barrington, to travel in the England team coach to the new concrete bowl, the Wankhede stadium. The crowd outside the hotel and the ground would have made many an English third division football club envious, but from my point of view a measure of anxiety was beginning to creep in. Still no sign of Bishen, and I had quickly assessed the position that once the game got under way the following morning it would be almost impossible to trap him alone.

Two nets were set up on opposite sides of the outfield. Around the one allocated to the Indian team a crowd of around 2000 had gathered. Out came their players in small groups, but still no Bedi. Then eventually the familiar 'patka' or turban, blue in colour, emerged from under the main stand. Alone. The applause began and steadily increased as the thickset figure of the Indian captain sauntered towards the net. It was difficult to hear each other speak as we greeted one another, he with a gentle, soft handshake accompanied by a languid, heavy-eyed look from those deep brown eyes. We made arrangements to meet that evening back at the hotel and Bedi strolled away to bowl to Viswanath, one of the more accomplished Indian batsmen. To a cricketer, standing behind a net gives one an odd perspective of the game. One's eyes are conditioned to making batting judgements at a range of twenty-two yards, and the combination of being some four or five yards further back and looking at the approaching bowler square on as opposed to the normal sideways batting position affects one's judgement. Yet I saw enough of Bedi, even in the relaxed, non-combative atmosphere of net practice, to reinforce all the opinions voiced by many of the world's finest batsmen that Bedi is the supreme exponent of the art of flight. His 'run-up' could hardly be described as such. It's more a sleek, catspaw pad up the wicket. A final slight skip to ease his body into the classical sideways-on position with the eyes looking unblinkingly down the wicket over the right shoulder, and with a rotation of the bowling arm as though on oiled castors the ball loops down towards the batsman.

It's a great action, faultless at every point, without a hint of strain or tension. From start to finish the rhythm and tempo, even at the end of a 60-over spell in temperatures approaching the 100 mark, remain at '*andantino con molto espressione*'! The smoothness of his action is why he has survived at the highest level for so long in a country where the wear and tear, not to mention intrigue, hasten cricketers if not actually into the grave at least into an early retirement. But to my mind there is no doubt that despite all his considerable natural gifts, Bedi would not have been as successful without an inner 'nirvana', or sense of peace. It radiates from everything he does. With his temperament and attitude he could never have been anything other than a slow bowler.

The man's whole philosophy is summed up in the way he runs up to bowl. It is said that animal lovers eventually get to look like their pets. If so, then Bedi is in love with the subtleties of spin bowling, mirrored in the way he looks, his method and his approach. Alone among the world's finest bowlers he will actually applaud a positive stroke from a batsman that sends the ball into the crowd for six, for he recognizes that in attack a class batsman is at his most vulnerable!

An accusation often levelled at the current lot of outstanding Indian spinners, who besides Bedi and Chandra include Prasanna and Venkataraghavan, is that they bowl on wickets specially prepared for them, which give turn from the first morning of a Test match. While this cannot be denied, it does not explain away the great success Bedi in particular has had abroad. His performances in the West Indies during the 1975/6 series on shirtfront wickets against the most powerful batting lineup in the world are remarkable. Three for 113 in 43 overs in the first Test; five for 82 in 34 overs and three for 44 in 36 overs in the second; three for 73 in 30 overs in the third, and two for 68 in 32 overs in the fourth. In the series, 200.5 overs for 456 runs and 17 wickets!

In the West Indies he revealed another side to his elusive character when, in the fourth and final Test, he called his batsmen from the field at Kingston with India only 12 runs ahead with five wickets remaining. With five men injured as a result of their first innings battering at the hands of Holding and Daniel, Bedi ceded the match rather than risk further injury to his team – an unprecedented gesture which showed either faint-heartedness or a hard core to the bland exterior of the Indian captain – it depends on your interpretation.

Our scheduled meeting at the Taj Hotel that February evening never transpired. An official reception, so beloved in India, got in the way, and so we postponed our get-together until the end of the first day's play. Fortunately for me, India won the toss and batted throughout, making 261 for 4, so Bedi was in a relaxed, contented frame of mind as I climbed the enormous staircase to his third-floor suite in the Taj. With characteristic generosity he ordered a meal for two to be served in his room, and opening two beers we started to talk.

But it was hopeless. The telephone never stopped ringing, with the callers begging for tickets, offering good luck charms, asking Bedi to come and have his picture taken at a local bazaar or just wanting to come up to the room to shake his hand. For short periods we were also joined by his great friends Viswanath, Chandrasekhar and Gavaskar, who had made a hundred earlier in the day. A trio of beautiful, saried women popped in to offer their congratulations ... it was like open day at the Casbah!

What I had not allowed for was the tempo and pattern of life in the East. Eventually the last guest disappeared, we opened another brace of beers, Bishen rang the desk to stop any more calls being put through for an hour, unwound his patka, and we settled down.

WALKER: Watching you bowl, Bishen, with that lovely lazy action of yours, it looks as if you came out of the cradle wheeling away and like Tennyson's brook will go on for ever. You must have started playing cricket at a very early age.

BEDI: Believe it or not, no. Normally in India boys begin playing in the streets and yards almost as soon as they can walk ... you saw them on the way back to the hotel from the ground. They use anything, bits of driftwood, pebbles ... a split tennis ball is a real luxury. I didn't have any real interest in the game until I was about twelve, and even then I didn't take it up voluntarily. I remember listening to the radio during a Test match between India and the West Indies at Kanpur in 1958. Gupte took nine wickets for 102 in one innings and suddenly, just like a revelation, I knew that was what I wanted to do. Up until then I'd tried to bowl fast because I'd taken up cricket to try to slim down. I'm not a natural athlete, and the boys at the St Francis High School in Amritsar used to tease me so much about being fat that I thought that by bowling fast I'd lose weight. I was – I suppose I still am – very sensitive about my size and bulk. But from the moment I changed to spinners I no longer regarded that as a problem and everything seemed to click. Within three years I was playing for the North Punjab in the Ranji trophy competition. When I was young I was a great watcher of bowlers and used to try to imitate them when I got home or in the nets. I remember seeing Tony Lock bowl chinamen and googlies when he was in India with Ted Dexter's team in 1961. I'd love to be able to bowl like that, but my skills lie elsewhere and it didn't take me long to realize this.

WALKER: Everyone in the game thinks of you as a bowler who relies principally on flight rather than spin. Looking at your hands now, you haven't got the characteristic hard callous or split inside part of your index finger of the great spinners of the ball, nor, despite the vast number of overs you bowl, is the

The Indian cobra

knuckle of your left-hand index finger enlarged as often happens to big spinners.
BEDI: Oh, I think I do spin the ball sufficiently. We don't play all our cricket in this country on rough tracks, as is sometimes believed abroad. Look at the huge scores we get in the Ranji trophy matches. I've found I can spin the ball enough to make it turn on most pitches but the reason why my fingers aren't like you describe is simple. I don't spin the ball from the same part of the finger as most other bowlers of my type. I don't screw the ball down deep into the split between my index and middle fingers, which is what most big spinners of the ball do for extra leverage. Because I try to beat the batsman in the air as much as off the pitch, it's important that I don't grip the ball too tightly, which would inhibit the flight as I release it. So I've developed a method of spinning the ball from the flat, ball part of the upper joint of my index finger. If you release the ball properly so that when it arrives at the other end it lands on the seam, then it'll turn providing the bounce of the ball gives it a chance to grip. If you bowl it too fast and flat, say like Derek Underwood, then on a good wicket it'll just skid through because it's not in contact with the ground long enough to get any real purchase.
WALKER: A lot of modern Test cricketers are remarkably ignorant about the history of the game. Have you much interest in the past?
BEDI: Oh yes. When I was at school I used to read every cricket book I could get my hands on. I remember books by Benaud, Bradman and particularly Wally Grout. I liked him because he seemed to have a nice sense of humour. I learnt a lot about the game from reading and then trying to put into practice what I absorbed. In a historical sense, yes I think I'm aware of the traditions of the game. Don't forget in India we still feel very close to events concerning English cricket and I know a bit about many famous players that have never visited India in my time – people like Hobbs and Verity and Hammond and Woolley. I certainly don't consider my interest in the game to be just as a player pure and simple.

WALKER: Almost from the time you entered first-class cricket you've known regular success right the way through up to Test match level. It must give you a warm glow of satisfaction to look back on your career.

BEDI: Well, yes. But I've always been mildly surprised by my achievements. You see, I never thought that I'd make it as a cricketer. I think it highly likely that had I not had early success when I began in top-class cricket in 1961, I'd have ended up in my father's business in the textile industry after perhaps doing a law degree at University. But once I got into the Indian Test side, well, all those thoughts just flew out of the window. When I was selected for India against the West Indies in 1966 it was the first Test match I'd ever seen! It was a very lonely experience, one I'll never forget. Our side was dominated by players from the west and south and it was difficult for a Punjabi like myself to be accepted. It was like this for a number of years, and consequently it helped to make me a rather shy and withdrawn person.

WALKER: Things have certainly changed since then. I'm thinking about what I've seen in the last few days, where your handling of the media and the inevitable hangers-on that are attracted to the game has been quite superb. How did this change come about?

BEDI: No doubt about it, it was my decision to come and play in England. When Northamptonshire approached me to join them in 1972 I jumped at the chance because I've always enjoyed bowling in UK conditions ... except when it's damn cold! Being involved in county cricket on a seven-day-a-week basis also brought me out as a person. It's very hard to get accepted in an English dressing-room; the average pro takes a long time to loosen up and you have to have considerable personal success before you really become part of the team. It took me a whole season to adjust. 1972 was a wet season and I had to modify a lot of my technique and especially my length on the slower wickets. But I love a challenge, and the one thing that five years on the county circuit has done is to improve my application and resolve to do well. I concentrate much better now than I used to used to as a youngster so that 40- or 50-over spells without a break aren't as exhausting as they might be.

WALKER: In your time you've bowled against all the best batsmen in the world today. Who are the ones that have impressed you?

BEDI: Let me say straight off that I don't accept that cricket is a game of chance. You make your own luck. I love a challenge and prefer to bowl at batsmen who are prepared to pit their skill against mine – players like Sobers and Richards. I know a few of today's bowlers who chicken out when they come face to face with Barry, but not me. I like to crowd him. Because he's such a good player on the offside I don't try to spin it too much when I bowl at him but rather try to vary the flight and width ever so slightly every ball. For me the greatest thrill in bowling is to have a batsman stumped. If you have achieved this you've really beaten him twice, in the air and off the wicket. By the way, I don't actually decide what kind of ball I'm going to deliver until I start my run-up. Sometimes I decide I'll bowl an arm ball, slightly quicker with very little spin. If the ball is still relatively new then it will probably swing in to the batsman in the air, particularly if I've delivered it from near the edge of the crease. I don't like to see a batsman play back. It usually means I've dropped it too short. The best back-foot player I ever came across was Ken Barrington; he's certainly the best defensive player I've met, but if you bowled a bad ball he hit it with such contempt that he gave you an inferiority complex! There are a lot of good players around these days who never make the international scene, but I can't think of any one player who stands out who isn't already acknowledged as a top-class Test batsman.

WALKER: Your action is so easy and relaxed you seem like an atomic clock to me ... on and on you go without losing either your length or line. Do you ever have days when things don't go quite right?

BEDI: Oh yes. My follow-through is very important. Unless I get my body rotating well and my left side swinging past the axis of my right hip, then things can go wrong with both my line and length. Like all slow bowlers I hate being cut or pulled, because it means somewhere along the line I've stiffened up or held on to the ball too long. I get really worried if I don't get the left hip working. I also concentrate, particularly when I'm starting a spell, on making sure that at the point of release my bowling arm is as high as possible. Once I've done this for an over or two it slips into the groove quite naturally. When I get tired, the ball of my front foot gets quite tender and although I look quite light on my feet, I get a fair amount of jarring in my hip on the follow-through, because I'm up on my toes a lot. Sometimes, after a really long spell, my shoulder gets sore, but I'm talking of sessions of 60 overs in a day or more! I'm not a muscular man but I've done a simple form of yoga most of my life and it certainly helps to keep me supple, oils the joints if you like. Another thing, I don't like bowling over the wicket to right-handers because I can't really get a good hip action going.

A lot of bowling is done in the mind. I think being an Indian helps me as a slow bowler. Off the field I'm a pretty calm sort of person. On it, I don't get too upset if umpires' decisions go against me or if catches are dropped off my bowling, but I do have a strong inner voice of personal criticism. I remember bowling badly against Essex on a turning wicket a couple of seasons ago. At teatime I apologized to our captain, but fortunately I later did drop one on a length to the number 11 batsman, who was caught in the gulley and we won by one run! But I was very angry with myself that day.

WALKER: Do you still get the same enjoyment from the game as you used to when you were breaking into first-class cricket?

BEDI: Not so much. Playing all the year round as I have in recent years, takes it out of me. Do you know, I've bowled around 5000 overs in the last three years. As to enjoyment? Well, I'd like to play international cricket for at least another three years, but to retain one's interest in this game it's important to be winning more than losing. Any sportsman at the top will tell you this. I don't like being beaten, and after a defeat I can be bad news at home that night. Ask my wife Glenn about it if you like. I met her in Melbourne during our tour there in 1968. She'd probably tell you that touring can be a very hazardous business! Although I've got a house in Northampton, India is the place where we'll eventually settle, though what I'm going to do when I stop playing I haven't yet worked out. I'd like to stay in the game in some capacity, but not as an administrator, rather a government employee involved in sports coaching.

WALKER: A lot of first-class cricketers I know are bad watchers of the game. Indeed, some hardly see a ball bowled except when they're batting or fielding. What are you like in this respect?

BEDI: Oh, I'm a terrible spectator. Normally I use the time off the field to write letters. In India I can get anywhere between forty and fifty a day, many of them abusive I'm afraid. In my country they're very generous when you're winning, but when you're down it's the captain who stops most of the bullets. In India the pressures are far greater on us than touring teams, and although cricket is one of the few ways in which a man without the right connections can make his mark in our society, once you've arrived at the top you've got to be looking all ways at the same time. That's one of the reasons why I'm so strongly in favour of our Players' Association. It's modelled on similar lines to the one in England, except that our main concern is to improve the lot of Indian international cricketers. Millions of rupees go into the Board's coffers from a Test series and yet we only get a couple of crumbs. The idea of our Association was originally 'Tiger' Pataudi's. There's always been a tremendous lack of communication between the administrators of Indian cricket and the players. I've always considered myself a player's man and I was once dropped from the Test team after giving you a very harmless television interview in England after we'd lost the series there in 1974. But I think we've managed to improve the financial arrangements a lot. When I played against England in 1967 I got 750 rupees (£44) per Test. Now it's 7000 (£410). That's progress. Players ought to be more important than officials, but having said that I think umpires ought to be paid a lot more than they do. They've got the most difficult job in the world in India and yet they only get 700 rupees (£22) for a Test. It's scandalous.

WALKER: What are the things that irritate you about cricket as it's played today?

BEDI: What I would call 'bad cricket'. That means ultra-defensive fields with the sole object of trying to stop runs rather than bowl people out. I don't like the modern fast bowler's intimidatory tactics; it's completely against the spirit of the game. In the West Indies Holding and Daniel were trying to hit us out, not get us out. Because of the big prize monies involved there's now more of an attitude to win at all costs rather than to win by using superior skills. I also regret the stalemate that exists between India and Pakistan at present. At Northampton I play under the captaincy of Mushtaq Mohammed, the Pakistan captain. I don't think I've got a closer friend in cricket. Isn't it strange that his country can produce so many good fast-medium bowlers and we can't? Perhaps it's because Pakistan is a Muslim country and Islam is a more aggressive philosophy than ours. I don't think the usual excuses of our diet and climate are the real reason. I wish more of my own Sikh tribe played cricket, because generally speaking we've got a slightly hostile attitude to things we do in competition with others. We could certainly do with a couple of fast bowlers, particularly in Australia. I think to win in Aussie is the hardest task in cricket. They're so arrogant, and they've got the skill to go with it. In my own way I try to help maintain the old values of the brotherhood of cricket by always having a drink with the opposition at the end of play. I have a very simple philosophy. When I stop enjoying the game I'll stop playing. Although I'm not as fit as I was four years ago, I still get a great deal of pleasure from playing. Spinners tend to mature late, so perhaps the best is yet to come!

Knott – the ever-present danger

Alan Knott

Class is something an experienced eye recognizes in an instant and when one cuts the real Alan Knott free from the many and varied contortions that he goes through out on the field thus baring his skills down to the bone, the class is all-apparent.

However, it is only by playing alongside him that the true wizardry of the England wicketkeeper can be properly appreciated. It's rather like hearing a Beethoven symphony on disc compared with actually being in the Royal Festival Hall! In 1964, the year of Knott's debut in the Kent side, I had a front-row seat. Together with Don Shepherd of Glamorgan, one of the best uncapped bowlers in English cricket at the time, I had been invited to play for an Invitation Eleven against Cambridge University in a one-day match. At Fenners we were introduced to Alan Knott, the only member of a near-international-strength team we did not already know. He had then only just made a permanent place for himself in the Kent Eleven but we had already heard of him. Indeed, it had filtered through on the county grapevine that Les Ames, himself a wicketkeeper of renown, believed that in eighteen-year-old Alan Philip Eric Knott, Kent had found the natural successor to Godfrey Evans in the England team. I was prepared to accept such a well-grounded objective assessment, but not Don Shepherd.

Don belonged to the 'old pro' hard school. Praise ran from Don's lips like molasses off a shovel. But one moment in an otherwise readily forgettable game changed his attitude completely. Shepherd used to bowl a brand of medium-fast offbreaks that on helpful wickets made him virtually unplayable. Not only was he one of the most accurate bowlers I've ever seen but his highly developed competitive instinct made him a great attacking bowler. Because of his speed and bounce off the pitch, wicketkeepers used to stand some eight to ten yards back. They never thought of stumping opportunities but looked instead for the flying outside edge from the ball that did not turn or the scramble down the legside to prevent byes when it did. It was a crude, non-classical, but a very effective 'stopping' technique.

When our turn came to field, a shower of rain had given the wicket just enough of a soaking to present Shepherd with the sort of purchase he thrived upon and he was soon brought into the attack. I used to field at short leg in the Glamorgan side, where I caught over 250 catches from his bowling alone, so the young Knott looked at me inquiringly, for he'd never seen Don bowl before. 'I'd stand well back if I were you' was my advice. He took it, at least for the first two overs, during which time the University batsman, realizing that his only hope of survival was to stand well out of his ground, did just that. This was too much for our wicketkeeper, and when Shepherd turned to bowl the second ball of his third over he found his keeper crouched over the bails.

'Shep' enjoyed a challenge and decided he'd put this youngster back in his place – ten yards behind the wicket. He bowled again, the ball pitched on a length, turned, lifted and hit the inside edge of the bat hard enough to deflect several degrees.

Anyone who has played the game, and particularly those who have attempted to keep wicket, will tell you that standing up to an offspinner on a turning pitch is the most difficult thing in the world. The batsman's body obscures your view, and so with each and every ball there comes a moment when you lose sight of it. Well, on this occasion not only did Alan catch the rising edge at shoulder height far away to his left, but he was quick enough to to return to flick off the leg stump bail as the batsman fell forward off balance with the effort of his stroke. Caught or stumped Knott bowled Shepherd – they were both out.

The over passed without further incident until Shepherd passed me on the way to his fielding position at mid-off. With a characteristic shake of his head, he said out of the corner of his mouth: 'That's the best bloody stumping I've ever seen, and as for the catch ... that wasn't an edge, he hit it hard enough to be a leg glance!' That split second between the ball leaving his hand and his wicketkeeper's answering response to the error he had forced from the batsman had transformed a sceptic into a lifelong admirer.

Since that incident took place fourteen years ago, this could be said of virtually everyone in the game. Rarely has a cricketer in such a vulnerable position as wicketkeeper been so universally admired as Alan Knott. It used to be said of Godfrey Evans that he kept his best for Tests and that he found the county circuit something of a bind. Such is Alan Knott's professional pride in his own performance that the man who walks out at Lord's is indistinguishable from the one keeping in a charity 'do' in Tilehurst, Kent.

He's a private inward-looking sort of man, extremely conscious of his own state of body and mind. A thoughtful person, one who carefully weighs the pluses and minuses of any proposition on or off the field. It came as no surprise to those who know him well that he was one of the first to 'follow the dollar' with the Kerry Packer circus. He did this not out of a sense of dissatisfaction with what the game was giving him at county, Test and touring level, but rather as a result of a careful evaluation of what it will mean financially to him and his family in the long run.

Yet for all his caution in material things there runs a strong streak of humour through his character. Being a wicketkeeper has probably helped to develop this side of his personality. Verbally, it's of a spikey, mickey-taking nature, but the barbs have a gentle tip and the smile is never far from the surface.

Much thought and practice have gone into the acquiring of

his splendid wicketkeeping technique. It hasn't happened by accident, it's definitely come about by design, giving an important clue to the reasons behind his success. Unlike the vast bulk of international sportsmen who are involved in games or competition involving a moving ball, very early in his career Alan Knott systematically evaluated his abilities and weaknesses. Instead of just being content to ride his inherent latent skills and allow the normal practising of his sport to suffice in terms of maintaining satisfactory levels of form and performance, he carefully weighed up what he should do in any given situation and then set out to create these conditions in pre-season or pre-match practice.

Watch him warm up in the outfield before the start of a day's play, and I don't mean the body-stretching exercises that have become so much his individual trademark. First he gets one or two of the fieldsmen to bowl at him, pitching the ball roughly where a length would be so that he gets into the rhythm of taking the ball at the peak of its rise. Then a short session of over-pitched balls, those nasty half-volleys that can be a wicketkeeper's nightmare, particularly when they land in the worn footmarks left by the bowlers. After this a few long throw-ins which get him used to the background of the particular ground, and then a short wind-up sequence of close catching with another member of the team to sharpen up the reflexes and agility.

These pre-match loosening-up sessions are very much part of Alan Knott's conditioning for the day that lies ahead, and it's because he's so thorough and disciplined with himself that he has lasted so long. His consistency is such that an England Eleven without him in the last ten years is unthinkable. He took just 78 Tests to overhaul Godfrey Evans' world record of 219 dismissals set in 91 matches, keeping in the main to attacks which on paper anyway were inferior to those of his illustrious predecessor in the Kent and England teams.

On a flying trip I made to Bombay to see the fifth and final Test against India in February 1977, he produced one moment, rather as he had at Fenners thirteen years earlier, which reconfirmed my belief that he is without peer in his craft. On the first day, India, already having lost the series, were grinding on towards a big first-innings total. Gavaskar made a hundred, but was overshadowed by a brilliant innings of 83 by Patel. With precious little incentive and only three wickets taken for 261, the England bowlers were looking dispiritedly towards the clock as it inched its way towards close of play. The temperature was near 100°F, the game virtually dead, the tour nearly over, there was nothing left to play for.

Tony Greig bowled the last over of the day. Third ball, Patel tried to drive Greig through the covers but instead got a thick inside edge which screwed the ball down past his leg stump. His back foot hardly left the ground, but in a tumbling split-second movement, Knott left-handed swept the ball into the wicket to gain the umpire's stumping decision. It was an inspired moment of concentration from a professional sportsman whose reactions were immediate despite the overall atmosphere of gloom and inevitability. Next day England took India's remaining six wickets for 77 runs and were very much back in the game. Had Patel survived the night before, India would in all probability have won the Test and knocked a lot of the gloss from a triumphant England tour of the subcontinent.

It would be an oversight to ignore Knott's contribution as a batsman. Not surprisingly, he's a fine player of spin bowling and a wristy cutter of anything short of a length. For a man of such slim stature predictably nicknamed 'Flea', he is surprisingly good against genuine pace – his century against the West Indians Roberts, Holding, Holder and Daniel at Headingley, Leeds, in 1976 was full of courage, resolution and no mean skill, and he's also had his high moments against Lillee and Thomson.

But it was natural that when we eventually sat down to talk in the physiotherapy room at Edgbaston, Birmingham, on the opening Sunday of the 1977 season as Kent started off on their defence of the John Player League Championship, our initial exchanges were all about wicketkeeping.

KNOTT: You'd never believe it, but I actually started as a quick bowler! Look at me now ... under ten stone and only a shade over five and a half feet, not exactly the ideal build for a budding Thomson or Holding is it, and can you imagine what I was like aged eleven? Like all children the idea of bowling fast and knocking the stumps flying was one of the game's biggest attractions. But my father, who was wicket-keeper for the Belvedere club near Woolwich, always used to encourage me to try my hand at all parts of the game.

It was only after I'd kept in the school versus staff game when I was fourteen that I began to keep wicket seriously. As a lad I used to go along to the Kent County nets where Claude Lewis and David Constant, now a Test umpire, were the coaches. Claude soon whispered to me that I was too small to bowl fast and suggested I should see if I could turn the ball. Indeed, Les Ames encouraged me to try offspinners because Kent were very short in this department, but then came one of those series of incidents that change a life. Derek Ufton, then the county's second eleven wicketkeeper, went to manage Plymouth Argyle football club, and after a winter in South Africa, Tony Catt, then the Kent number one, suddenly decided to emigrate there. So in 1964 I found myself the only wicketkeeper on the staff, and luckily I took to it immediately. But like everyone else, I wasn't too happy standing up at the start of my career ... I had a natural fear of being hit in the face.

WALKER: That's interesting, because speaking from memory, I think you've hardly missed a dozen matches through injury in thirteen years. Is this because you've been luckier than others or is your technique and pre-match preparation better and more thorough than most?

KNOTT: I think I'm luckier, indeed aside from breaking my middle finger during the 1975 World Cup plus a few other common-day bumps and bruises, I can't remember a really serious injury. As to technique. Well, yes, without being

Everything is possible

immodest I think I've got a good method because I always make sure that I take the ball with my fingers at right-angles to the oncoming ball. Wicketkeepers suffer far fewer injuries these days for two reasons. The equipment's much better, and now hardly anyone stands up to medium-pacers. In the days when they did, like between the wars, there were any number of broken knuckes and fingers, nearly all of them as a result of the tradition of standing up to anyone who was a fraction slower than genuinely fast. It was a stupid example of pride if you like; it was considered a sign of 'weakness' if you stood back. You know as well as I do that a so-called 'medium-pacer' lets the ball go at around seventy miles per hour. Fast bowlers in the Lillee, Snow and Holding mould aren't much more than twenty mph quicker. The wear and tear on old wicketkeepers' hands was terrible. I remember the first time I met Herbert Strudwick, the old Surrey and England keeper. He had an amusing habit of starting every sentence with the expression 'Oooh'. After he'd gone I asked an old player why he did this. 'Oh,' he said, 'it's a legacy from his wicketkeeping days. When he came off the field he used to gently ease his hands out of his gloves and to soothe away the aches and pains he would put them alternately into basins of hot and cold water. The "Oooh" came each time he had to dip them into the hot! It's a habit that stuck with him for life.' That won't happen to me. Look at my hands. They're the same shape I was born with and I intend to go to the grave with them like that.

WALKER: This indicates to me that you must have some pretty positive views on wicketkeeping gloves and the way they're made. What about the ones that carry your name? Did you have anything to do with their design or is it purely a royalty arrangement that you have with the manufacturers?

KNOTT: Oh no. I took a long time examining other keepers' equipment and trying out different makes before I allowed my name to go on a pair. I'm a great believer in protection. Every finger end should have a stoll – a hard rubber cap which deflects most of the impact of a blow on the ends of the fingers. I also believe in having substantial, strong leather backs to my gloves. Although I'm obviously not going to be hit there, I find that this helps to keep the palm cup at the front of the glove in position. I know a lot of first-class keepers prefer softer, more pliable gloves, but not for me; the firmer, the stouter, the better. Ideally I like to take away all sensation of the ball entering my hands. I'm not a 'feel' wicketkeeper in this sense. I'm looking to make my gloves into a cricketing equivalent of a baseball mitt. For instance, Rodney Marsh often practises with one of these simply because they give his hands so much more cover. I'm for protection all the way.

Another thing, I always wear two pairs of inner gloves and keep them for as long as possible once they're broken in. I never wet them. I know this is a popular idea amongst club cricketers and schoolboys but I find this doesn't help cushion the impact at all, and wet inners also tend to make the outer glove slide around. Since the 1970 tour of Australia I've always put bits of surgical tape around my little fingers to prevent bruising. John Murray of Middlesex used to bind all his fingers, but I find with my own gloves and decent chamois leather inners, the little fingers which take the brunt of the impact are the only ones I need do. Sometimes, particularly if I've had a few weeks off between seasons or tours, I tape a strip of sponge rubber to the inners along the base of my fingers. As to the gloves themselves, when they're new I spend hours working the space between the thumb, index and middle fingers into a shaped cup. That's where most catches are caught, and if you can form a deep cup then even if you don't quite catch it in the right part of the hand, it'll still stick. Incidentally, I also insist on a strong wide web between thumb and forefinger for this reason.

WALKER: You're known in the game as very much a thinking cricketer. What modifications if any have you made to your approach because of one-day cricket?

KNOTT: If I can, I always stand back in the Sunday League programme. I'm terrified of letting four byes go down the legside. It's a wicketkeeper's nightmare, because so many sides are about on a par these days that we're getting more and more limited-over games lost by just a couple of runs. If, say, I've let eight byes through, this could cost us the game. In any case, there are so few stumpings in modern cricket generally that I don't see the point of standing up just because the bowler's on the slow side. Another thing. By standing back I can partially make up for the absence of first slip and leg slip. Because I'm light on my feet I cover a fair amount of ground either way and can reach balls I'd have no chance with standing up. Incidentally, I spend a lot of time practising one-handed catching. It's vital to be able to do this. Because I'm stronger pushing off with my right leg I can dive further to my left, and so I'm a little better down the legside one-handed than diving in front of first slip.

WALKER: I wouldn't dare suggest that you're not in your prime – after all you're still only thirty-one, despite the fact you've played in over eighty Test matches. But looking back, is there any one part of your career when you feel you were at your best?

KNOTT: Oh, that's easy. I think the Indian tour of 1972 was the high point. During the English summer that preceded it I didn't think I'd performed anywhere near my full potential. I'll be honest, I was worried by the way I slipped into a couple of small bad habits ... I didn't always look at the ball, I found myself stretching for balls outside the leg stump ... a sure sign that I wasn't moving fast enough on my feet. You know, there's just that niggling knowledge that things aren't going really well. Perhaps the fact that I had one of my best seasons with the bat might have had something to do with it. Keeping wicket requires a fantastic amount of concentration, it's by a long way the most taxing position on the field, and I think my own wicketkeeping form suffered as a result of the time I was spending at the batting crease.

So before going to India I sat down and thought out the problem. I knew it was going to be a tour where I'd be standing up a lot more than in England because of the wickets, and that the heat, dust and glare would make life that much more difficult. In the end I think it all boiled down to concentration and plenty of rest. We play far too much cricket in this country; we're at it virtually every day from May to September. On a tour you can relax, get away from the game so that when you actually go out on the field you're in the right frame of mind. It was also a good tour in the sense that we had a captain with flair – Tony Lewis. He was the right sort of man for India, and although we didn't win the series he created the right kind of atmosphere ... at least for me ... to bring out my best. I think it was in India that I really first learnt how to relax. I do it by keeping my body in motion. It's not nerves that cause me to wave my arms around and do knee bends. I do it to keep everything supple and on the move. I've found it's the best way to unwind.

WALKER: I'm glad you brought that up, because you've got more little mannerisms than any other contemporary player I know. Do you also have fads about food or exercise?

KNOTT: I think it's important to understand that there's a reason behind everything I do. It's not just a question of being superstitious or having odd beliefs. You may not think it but I'm a very stiff person, and that's why I exercise as often as I do out on the field to keep loose. Off it I'm completely different from what most people imagine. I take my time, sleep a lot in the dressing-room and just generally mooch around. I'm certainly not a bundle of energy. The vital muscles in a wicketkeeper are those in the groin and hamstring, and I keep stretching these out on the field to keep them toned up. I watch my diet ever since an American health expert advised me that for maximum energy output I should eat natural foods only – that means no artificial preservatives. It's certainly worked in my case, because since I've stuck to his diet, which is now round about five years, I've felt much fitter and certainly had more zip.

WALKER: A lot of up-and-coming wicketkeepers model themselves on you. Presumably you were the same when you started out in the first-class game thirteen years ago. Whom did you admire?

KNOTT: Jimmy Binks of Yorkshire was the best keeper I've ever seen. He had such marvellous hands, the ball just seemed to melt into them, and standing up he was simply incredible. I never saw him drop a ball! I learnt a lot from watching Jimmy and also looking at and talking to Keith Andrew of Northamptonshire. He was another fine keeper. I remember I was having a lot of trouble catching the ball cleanly when I was standing up. After watching Jimmy and Keith it suddenly came to me why. I was trying to catch it with my knees still bent in a half crouch ... incidentally I always crouch down because it helps to keep my back supple and therefore relaxed. Anyway, I noticed that they both straightened their knees just before the ball arrived and so got them out of the way, allowing their hands and elbows plenty of room to move. When I tried it, it worked immediately. I also had a lot of encouragement from Les Ames, who I never saw keep in a first-class game, and of course Godfrey Evans. He was so strong – just like Rodney Marsh who's got legs as thick as my chest! It's such an advantage to be strong, particularly in the legs. If you've got power there it's so much easier to correct a mistake, and they also absorb a lot of fatigue. Wasim Bari of Pakistan is the best international wicketkeeper around at the moment. He hasn't Marsh's strength but he's so quick and agile and he's got marvellously safe hands. He concentrates well too. He found, as I did in India during that series in 1972 we were discussing earlier, that not talking a lot out on the field helped him concentrate that much harder. One thing that surprises me in these days where so much keeping is done standing back is why there aren't more tall stumpers! I'd love to be six inches or more taller. Providing you're supple I don't think it matters a jot how tall you are. And if you've got longer arms then of course you can reach catches you otherwise wouldn't lay a glove on.

WALKER: What attitude do you think has helped most towards making you the class keeper you are?

KNOTT: Two things, actually. I'm a patient person, that helps a lot. I also work hard at my game. I realized before the Indian tour of 1972 that I couldn't rely on my ability alone. This kind of self-analysis is very important. You can take in any amount of good advice but it's the advice you give to yourself that sinks in deepest. I think if you're a wicketkeeper you've got to believe that every ball is coming to you. It's also important to try for everything and to practise diving catches both left and right until they become instinctive.

WALKER: On a broader basis, you must have played with many cricketers all over the world who have left a deep impression on you.

KNOTT: Oh, yes. Where do I begin? Well, just a couple ... The best bowler I've kept to is John Snow. In Australia in 1971 he was quick and so accurate. Every time he bowled a bouncer it was right on target. Overseas, he was able to move the ball both in the air and off the wicket, and that's a rare thing indeed. If anything he was a better bowler abroad than in England, and he's a marvellous bloke. Despite his public image of irresponsibility I've always found him very sensible. On the other hand, Jeff Thomson is certainly the quickest bowler I've ever faced. He could, before his shoulder injury really nobbled him, get the ball up off a length like no one else I know. He was the sort of bowler who could produce a ball to bowl even Sobers if he had 150 on the board! Dennis Lillee is a terrific fast bowler with such a great heart, and the most underrated bowler I've ever played against is also an Australian, offspinner Ashley Mallett. He spun it a lot and had a deceptive flight, but of course he always played in the shadow of his country's fine fast bowlers.

When it comes to captains, two men stand out. Brian Close. He's terrific. A real 'iron man' and yet he treated me so carefully and with great gentleness when I first came into Test cricket. 'Closey' always led by personal example. I've never come across any player so completely sure that he was right and that in the end he and his team would come out on top. Ray Illingworth's the other. He and Brian are very similar, except that Ray is even better when it comes to understanding the needs of his players. He knows that each cricketer is a different kind of human being with varying needs and he adjusts his approach accordingly to get the best out of them.

WALKER: You've lived for the past ten years at the very top of your profession. How long can you continue to withstand the considerable pressures without losing either your form or interest?

KNOTT: I'm a bit of a pessimist. I've got a lot from the game, a good benefit and the rest, but I've also put in my fair share too. I could go any time. That's in part why I signed for Packer. A bad injury, a loss of flair – that's possible you know with all the cricket we play. It can become a drag. Playing Test matches is an exhilarating pleasure providing you're doing well. I couldn't imagine returning to play club cricket;

maybe table tennis or golf, but not cricket. Once you've touched the heights in a particular sport anything else at a lower level in the same sport becomes something of a personal compromise. Patient and placid though I may be, I don't think I've got the temperament or desire to accept the descent.

A good batsman, too, against genuine pace

Turner – the end of a long, long month

Glenn Turner

Worcester cricket ground deservedly takes its place as the most photographed and arguably the most beautiful cricket ground in all England. Yet for me, on a balmy midsummer day during the 1967 season, it was one of the most unappealing places on earth. I was leaning back against the boundary railings as a quite dreadfully meaningless second eleven game inched towards an inevitable draw. Recovering from an injury, I had gone to Worcester to play for Glamorgan seconds in a warmup game. The shirtfront batting wicket and convivial social life of Worcester were supposed to have extraordinary therapeutic qualities for cricketers like myself who were searching for confidence and form!

The reason for the greyness of this particular day's cricket occupied the crease for nearly four hours while making 30 runs. Oblivious to the needs of the game or the entreaties of a succession of batsmen who passed to and from the middle, dying in a vain attempt to open up the match for a declaration, twenty-year-old Glenn Turner from Dunedin in the South Island of New Zealand remained unmoved, lost in his own private world of concentration.

My, how times have changed. Ten years later the name Turner is synonymous with some of the most exhilarating limited-over batting, with strokes on the offside that have drawn comparisons with Hammond, Graveney and Cowdrey!

There can be no doubt that for all its critics, the shortened game of fixed-over duration cricket has been the making of Glenn Turner. Necessity and a personal realization that he would have to adapt to its needs rather than the other way round broadened and altered both his technique and his attitude, so that he is now one of the most attractive opening batsmen in world cricket.

Dunedin is hardly the 'Sin City' of the South Island. Colonized by some of the dourest and most hardbitten of Scottish settlers, their descendants remain as traditionally sombre and grey as much of the year's weather, a mere 900 miles from Antarctica. They're a close-knit community and, although it is mere conjecture on my part, perhaps in his roots lay Glenn's initial cricketing problems in this country. First he had to battle to survive and to make a breakthrough in first-class cricket and secondly and of parallel importance, he had to convince others that he had it in him to become an integral part of an English county cricket team. This is not so easy as it sounds. Petty jealousies abound in dressing-rooms, just as lifelong friendships are often forged through years traipsing around the first-class grounds of England and Wales.

Despite his present freedom, a lot of South Islander determination still characterizes Turner's batting; like his watchful stance, with the left hand wrapped well around the top of the handle in an ultra-defensive grip. It remains one of modern cricket's great mysteries how he manages to hit the ball so hard through the covers. Any worthwhile coaching manual will say that with his grip it's impossible to get the free swing of the bat necessary to belt the ball through the offside with any power. Turner is the exception that proves an otherwise hard and fast rule, but he must have an extremely flexible left wrist, because there are few more positive or harder drivers of the ball in the game at the moment. Then there is the cautious, almost suspicious tapping of the bat at the crease. The whole stance is one of watchfulness and, if he'll pardon the analogy, rather that of an expectant praying mantis! He's one of those opening batsmen who really 'smell' the ball. Not for him the desperate slash outside the off stump. Turner lets the ball come on to him, playing it at the last possible moment.

It's a method which has brought him considerable success at all levels of cricket. He has carried his bat through two Test innings. His 223 not out against the West Indies at Kingston, Jamaica, in 1971/2 was the highest score ever made by a player batting throughout an innings, and at twenty-two years sixty-three days he was the youngest man ever to do so. (During that highly successful tour, which really established him as an opener of true international class, he batted for 705 minutes in the Georgetown Test while scoring 259!) Against England in 1969 at Lord's in the second Test, his 43 not out was gathered out of a total of 131. More recently, in June 1977, his innings of 141 out of Worcestershire's total of 169 against Glamorgan represented 83.63 per cent of the runs made by his team, the highest percentage ever recorded! And he is one of only ten batsmen who have scored two centuries in a match on four occasions.

But if Glenn Turner, still the somewhat shy man from Dunedin even after a decade of being in cricket's front line, has something really to shout about, it must surely be his achievement of scoring 1000 runs by the end of May in 1973. In eleven matches for the touring New Zealanders between 24 April and 31 May he aggregated 1018 runs from innings of 41, 151*, 143, 85, 7, 8, 17*, 81, 13, 53, 44, 153*, 3, 2, 66*, 30, 10*, and 111, at an average of 78.30. In those thirty-eight days he did what no man since the war, not even Hutton, Bradman, Hammond, Compton, May, Cowdrey or Boycott, have managed to do. Indeed, before Turner, the last man to achieve this stupendous feat of skill and endurance was Bill Edrich back in 1938! In the whole colourful history of the first-class game, which stretches back nearly 120 years, only eight men have ever achieved 1000 before the end of May: Bradman twice in 1930 and 1938; Hammond, who in 1927 scored 1042 runs in just twenty-two days; Grace, 1016 in the same number of days in 1895; Charlie Hallows, perhaps the most remarkable of them all, for on the last day of May 1928 he needed 232 against Sussex at Old Trafford (he got them and was out next ball!); Tom Hayward – the 'Glenn Turner' at the beginning of this century who averaged 96.6 as he reached 1074 by the end of May 1900; and finally Bill Edrich in 1938, the same year as Bradman's second scaling of this batting Everest. Edrich got the ten runs he needed during the final day's play of Middlesex's game against the Australians, and by an odd twist of fortune and the fixture list he scored all his 1010 runs at his home ground, Lord's!

What is significant looking at that list of cricketing immortals is that besides Turner only Bradman is an overseas player.

The gap between Bill Edrich in 1938 and Glenn Turner in 1973 is thirty-five years, and with the present structure of first-class cricket it must be highly probable that Turner's will be the last name entered in this particular section of a batting Valhalla.

Like many of the overseas importations into first-class cricket in the United Kingdom during the 1960s, Turner was first spotted by an English professional on a winter coaching assignment. In his case it was Billy Ibadulla, the small but resolute Pakistani Test all-rounder who played with much distinction and no little charm for Warwickshire between 1954 and 1972. Ibadulla had spotted the thin, undersized Turner at Otago Boys High School, and together with that talented New Zealander Bert Sutcliffe had coached and encouraged the young man. It was Ibadulla who suggested to Turner that he had what it takes to make the grade in English first-class cricket and promised to organize a trial with Warwickshire should Turner ever find his way to the United Kingdom.

Soon after leaving school Turner entered the twilight world of insurance, but soon found the sporting call too strong to resist and after working for eighteen months at night in a bakery to earn extra money towards his fare, he eventually saved enough to book a one-way ticket. Then a matter of days before he was due to leave came a letter from Warwickshire regretting the fact that as they had now taken on their quota of overseas players they could not offer him any prospect of employment! The impact hit Glenn with the force of a blow to the solar plexus, but that broad streak of resilience that was to characterize his early tottering steps in first-class cricket made him climb the steps into the plane despite the bad news. Conscience-stricken Warwickshire arranged trials for him at Worcestershire, Lancashire, Middlesex and Surrey.

He got no further than his first two-day stint at New Road, Worcester. The talent was there, no doubt about it. It was instantly recognizable, and most importantly Worcester had room for him on their staff.

That was in 1967, the year that I spent those frustrating hours on the boundary edge while the twenty-year-old ground the soul out of that second eleven game. I remember talking in the bar afterwards to Dick Richardson, the former Worcestershire and England batsman, who also played in that game. 'He'll never make it,' I said. 'He hasn't got either the strength or the will to hit it off the square.' This snap judgement on my part proved to be as accurate as the time I suggested to a young student at Witwatersrand University, Johannesburg, that he try some other game because he didn't have it in him to be anything other than an ordinary club cricketer. Two years later Eddie Barlow was probably the best white all-rounder in the world!

Yet in a way I could have been right about Glenn. If it hadn't been for the frantic demands of the then newly introduced John Player Sunday League competition – this was in 1969, a year after his debut in English first-class cricket – then it is certainly possible that Glenn Maitland Turner would have survived a couple of seasons and then disappeared down under, reappearing in this country every five years or so as just another modestly endowed New Zealand opening batsman.

The transformation, one could almost go so far as to say the 'seeing of the light', occurred during an early season Sunday match against Northamptonshire. Opening the batting he took 34 overs to make 40 runs, and so completely bogged down Worcestershire's efforts that they were totally outplayed by a far weaker team. The lesson, aided by some pointed dressing room comment from players he had come to deeply respect, his present captain Norman Gifford, Tom Graveney and Basil d'Oliveira, sunk in. The following week against Essex he hit a rapid 60 which included five fours over the bowler's head ... virgin territory for Turner until that moment!

It took great strength of character to throw off the chains of caution which seemed at the time to be earning him a fingertip hold on a permanent place in the county team. Failure when you're young and unknown can often put back one's development by a couple of seasons. Twelve thousand miles from home the fear of failure and the cancellation of his summer's contract must have loomed like a vast spectre in the Turner subconscious. That he took such an enormous gamble in an alien and sometimes hostile environment speaks volumes for his strength of character.

From this point on, his career has been well documented, and it progressed rapidly until he was made captain of New Zealand in 1976. Equally important is his absorption into the English summer scene, where he makes a regular point of carrying on the best traditions of the old-style county cricketer ... play it hard on the field but always play it fair and then share a beer or two in the bar afterwards with the opposition.

He's one of a dying breed in this respect, but perhaps because of his upbringing he's at heart a traditionalist. His stay in Britain has also expanded his own brand of self-deprecatory humour. He now can recall with a grin running himself out when 99 looking for the single that would have given him a Worcestershire record of ten centuries in a season. The man he tried to take the run to was Clive Lloyd! That was during the 1970 season, and completely in character he did eventually go on to set the record.

I've always found him an engaging companion, a man with

a serious and critical side to his nature, but one who hasn't lost sight of the fact that cricket is, after all, a game and not an obsession. Because he spends more time at the crease in a season than many of us spend in a career, it was natural that our talk turned to batting.

WALKER: Along with Geoff Boycott you probably spend more time at the crease than any other contemporary cricketer. Do you love batting so much that you never lose your grip on the powers of concentration?

TURNER: Actually, I find it very difficult to concentrate. I will admit that once I've got over the first twenty minutes or so it gets easier – at least for the next couple of hours, but then as one gets physically tired and the bowlers present fewer problems it is possible to get 'forgetful'. By that I mean one lets little technical errors creep in, one begins to anticipate where one's going to hit the next ball before the bowler's actually released it, and one thinks too far ahead to a coming target, say an approaching hundred. This is dangerous, for of course the real priority is the ball which is about to be delivered to you. It's at this point during a long innings that I have to mentally shake myself and say: 'Come on now, concentrate on this one ball only.' To succeed in batting, at least to bat for a long time, I firmly believe that a batsman has to clear his mind completely midway through the bowler's run-up. He must rely on his conditioned reflexes to do the job when the ball's actually on its way. There isn't time for considered thought, and if a batsman attempts to weigh up all the possibilities before acting, it's too late – the ball's through him.

WALKER: Yours is a phenomenal record of survival, particularly against the new ball. Just how do you approach an innings?

TURNER: For me the most important thing is to play as few balls as possible early on. The more I can leave alone, the quicker I can assess the pace of the pitch, the amount of bounce in the wicket – a vital point this – and how much the ball will swing and move off the turf on that given day. Then I run a series of checks on my grip and stance. I make sure that my bodyweight is slightly forward on to my left foot. But to me the most important thing is to get my head into the right position and to keep it still. Balance is crucial in cricket, no more so than in batting in the Number 1 position, where late adjustments have to be made to cater for the moving ball. I try to keep my head tilted slightly forward as I find this helps to keep balance; if one's weight goes back, then it's impossible to stay in control of one's movements. Mentally I say to myself: 'Let the ball come, let the ball come.' There's a great tendency to instinctively thrust at the ball in an impulsive nervous way when one first goes in. I think this gets more people out than those who are genuinely beaten by a good ball. Once I'm in, then I have to keep restraining myself not to attempt to do too much. I know that if I bat a whole session, even if I'm not playing well or don't see a great deal of the strike, I should have added another 50 or so to my total. Three sessions a day equals 150 runs, not a bad day's work I think you'll agree. I tend to aim at targets like this: 40 has always been an important landmark for me – once I've got there, at least I've made a reasonable score. It's also the launching pad for a really big innings.

WALKER: Do you ever get tired, physically tired, of batting?

TURNER: I get more tired these days than I used to. I've been playing cricket now for nearly twelve months of the year for the past three years. I really could do with a break, and I'm going to take one in the winter of 1977/8, during which I'll stay in Worcester to organize my benefit season. There are so many other things in life that are worthwhile besides hitting a ball with a bat! I think this realization has made me less determined to occupy the crease come what may. Like Geoff Boycott, I used to hate getting out, and it would take me a couple of hours to get over it. I've grown out of that now, matured I like to think. I no longer lose any sleep if things aren't going well on the field.

WALKER: Have you an absolute faith in your own ability?

TURNER: I don't suppose there's any first-class batsman who hasn't. You just don't succeed without this inner belief. In all modesty, I don't think I often get beaten by a bowler; it's more a mistake of mine which has got me out. I don't worry about a bowler's reputation. Obviously one respects people like Tommy Cartwright, Derek Underwood and John Snow, but if you don't think you've got one more trick than they up your sleeve, then they've done you before you've even taken strike.

WALKER: Like all very good players, you seem to have a very sweet-sounding bat.

TURNER: Since I've been in this country I've used a variety of bats; it all depends who I'm contracted to. They're all much of a muchness at the top of the range. For a long time when I first came into the game I used bats made by Duncan Fearnley, the former Worcestershire player – one of the few craftsmen left in the trade. He literally made me my bats with the exactness of a Savile Row tailor. If I got a dud, he took it straight back and exchanged it. My bats are on the heavy side, around the 2lb 9oz mark with most of the thickness of the wood in the middle. As to other equipment, I nearly always wear a cap because it helps to shut out distracting movements around the field as well as the glare, and my gloves have a lot of extra padded webbing between the fingers of my right hand because I get hit a lot in this area. This is bound to happen if you get right behind the lifting ball.

WALKER: Where do you get most of your runs?

TURNER: When I first started, I used to get two thirds of my runs on the legside, but the county bowlers didn't take long to work that out so I've had to change my whole method. Now the reverse is true, but I think any top-class batsman must be able to score on both sides of the wicket; it all depends on how they bowl at you. Batting, like professional golf, is a game of percentages. I don't hook very often because I don't think I can be sure enough where the ball's going to go after I've hit it. So I sway out of the way of bouncers rather than play at them, or duck, without taking my eyes off the ball. When I was starting, I used to try tremendously hard to model myself on players like Colin Cowdrey and Tom Graveney. Now I go my own way, but their methods and application were considerable early influences on my career.

WALKER: If I can take you back to that May of 1973, the month when you scored all those runs. You must have been under a fair amount of strain, particularly from the press, who made a real meal of the fact that you looked like being the first man since Bill Edrich in 1938 to get 1000 before May was out. Looking back, did it make the task more difficult?

TURNER: To be honest, I was a little annoyed with people's preoccupation with this record but I don't think it made things harder for me. Things like that are of only passing interest anyway. We'd been lucky to play on some good wickets against some fairly friendly bowling up till that point. The weather was the crucial factor really, the 1000 runs strictly relative to how the team was doing as a whole. I'd got a lot of runs in the West Indies, but that was always in match-saving situations – not really the most satisfying way to play cricket. It was a bit like that playing for New Zealand in that 1973 tour.

WALKER: As the man who has to face the world's fastest bowlers, always when they're fresh, I suppose protective equipment is a pretty important part of your armoury if I can put it that way?

TURNER: You can never have too much of it ... providing it's not too heavy or bulky. There've been some enormous strides in this field in the last ten years. Starting with bats. There are deep edged bats, bats with scooped out backs for extra driving power, bats with carbon fibre handles for improved whip, even bats with holes in them! I think they're mostly gimmicks, and designed more for the television camera than the player. Pads are very important. Not surprisingly, because if someone like Wayne Daniel, Michael Holding or Dennis Lillee is letting 'em go at around ninety miles an hour you've only got around about one fifth of a second from the time he lets it go eighteen yards away to the time you hit it or it hits you. If I miss it with my bat, I don't want to be cut in two by the ball! As you can see, I'm not a very thickset guy, and when I get hit I stay hit for a long, long time. So I look for pads which have a good inner bolster running from the top of the knee down to the instep. Plastic or buckskin on the outside, it doesn't really matter except buckskin's more hard-wearing, although plastic needs less maintenance – you just wipe them with a damp cloth and they're clean. Then I always wear a thigh pad on my left leg, and sometimes a towel tucked down the inside of the right thigh too if the ball's moving around a lot. You know as well as I do how painful a blow there can be.

WALKER: I certainly do. I carry the scars to this day!

TURNER: My thigh pad is made of a light, shatterproof plastic material under which I put a piece of sponge rubber. This helps to absorb the shock. It still stings but doesn't bruise, and that's the thing that can really cripple you or slow you up. I've seen many players get out within a ball or two after taking a really painful blow on the thigh. They don't give themselves enough protection and haven't really recovered by the time the next ball's bowled. Then gloves. I've got a pair of these all-in-one-piece gloves. They're not bad, but I still prefer the old individual sausage-style horsehair-stuffed gloves with the extra padding I mentioned earlier. But they must be very flexible. Of course there's a box, padded around the edges, not hard plastic – must protect one's social life, old man – and finally boots. I always bat in spikes. A lot of good batsmen I know use crepe or rubber soles on hard, firm wickets. But I'm always afraid I'm going to slide or slip, so I always opt for spikes, even in India and the West Indies. Oh, one other thing. Although I don't go along with Mike Brearley's idea of a sort of plastic helmet underneath a normal cap, I do take his point about the dangers of facing really fast bowlers. But I think I'd find it very difficult to adapt to, far too hot and sticky if you're playing a long innings. It could put me off ... I'd be wondering if my headpiece had slipped if the cameras were on me ... and after all, I haven't got as much to protect as Mike, who was a first-class scholar at Cambridge!

WALKER: You're only thirty now. Do you see your life continuing as it is for many years to come?

TURNER: I enjoy playing for Worcestershire, and hope to go on with them for as long as they want me. I used to coach in Otago, now I've moved to the North Island. I find coaching very satisfying, but I prefer teaching adults, mind you. I'm not too fussed about trying to pass on basic skills – I enjoy discussing the finer, more individual points – but it's enjoyable nevertheless. I've interests in property development back home so I suppose it's well-nigh certain I'll eventually go back there to live. Certainly my fishing and shooting interests are better catered for in New Zealand than here. But at the moment, England has everything to offer. Outside of cricket I like most kinds of music. I used to find it difficult to relax but now I take my record player around the country and with Beethoven and Frank Sinatra to help, this has made a tremendous difference. I also like a few gin and tonics at the end of a day's play. And I also enjoy the company of my fellow players.

In my view a lot of a man's true character comes out on the field. I don't see any reason for a man to have one personality on the field, another off. It's very important to me to be judged and liked as a man, not as someone who happens to play cricket well, but who's a nasty bit of work off the field. Life's much bigger and broader than that.

D'Oliveira: 'cometh the hour. . .'

Basil d'Oliveira

The sun beat down from a washed-out denim-blue sky. It was New Year's Day, 1959, and the Natalspruit ground in one of the non-European suburban areas of Johannesburg was full of expectant black faces. They were there to see a rare event in the South Africa of nearly twenty years ago – a multiracial game of cricket. Not that the teams were integrated. That would have been too much for either the authorities to swallow or the Race Relations Act to accommodate. This was a match between a South African non-European Eleven and a team of professional cricketers who were in the Republic coaching during the English off-season. The pitch we were to play on was a jute mat tightly stretched over red gravel, and not a blade of grass was to be seen anywhere, even on the outfield. On such a surface, within three overs a new cricket ball looked as if it had been worked over on a sanding machine and the merest nudge through the covers seemed to accelerate over the rock-hard surface to the boundary. I led the team of professionals augmented by a former South African Test batsman, Ken Funston, then one of very few home-grown cricketers prepared to risk public scorn by associating with and competing against anyone other than sportsmen of pure European descent.

The game had first been mooted two months earlier, after I had been approached by a wealthy Johannesburg Indian about the feasibility of staging a match between the best cricketers of his race – very few black Africans play cricket – and a group of English coaches. Mr Patel was shrewd enough to appreciate that it would be well-nigh impossible to get a team of white South Africans of comparable strength to agree to play, but as many of the English pros who spent winters coaching in South Africa also taught at non-European schools, they would certainly be more approachable.

It's a big country, but it took only a few telephone calls and a couple of explanatory letters for me to gather a side together. Mr Patel's problems were more substantial. It was easy to select his team, but his choice of ground was limited to the only one allocated to non-Europeans in the whole city! Then he had to get past the formidable bastion of the Bureau for Race Relations. Eventually, after a great deal of detailed questioning, permission was granted subject to certain conditions. There was to be no fraternizing between the teams; no shared dressing room/shower/toilet facilities; and of course, no liquor to be taken into the ground! The strictures were irksome and to the English cricketers unnecessary, but without our compliance the game would not receive official permission, so room for negotiation was somewhat limited. With all this settled, I began to look forward to the game with special interest.

For a number of years it had been rumoured that in Cape Town lived a cricketer of Cape Malay extraction who but for the colour of his skin would almost certainly be a member of the Springbok team. It was a legend that had a touch of Rider Haggard about it ... a sort of cricketing male equivalent of 'She'. The Cape is an altogether more liberal area of South Africa than the Transvaal, and this Malay had played one or two matches against whites on grass wickets there with substantial success. His appearance in Johannesburg as captain of a non-white South African representative team was a rare thing needing a special police pass to allow him to travel outside his home city of Cape Town.

The details of our game are unimportant, except to say that the coaches' team, which included a fair sprinkling of county players not far off Test standard, was defeated, and thoroughly beaten at that.

What sticks in my memory is the first sight of that cricketer extraordinaire, Basil d'Oliveira. He made only 20-odd in each innings and took a couple of wickets with his medium-pace offspinners which bit and lifted on the matting wicket, but the impression he left was an indelible one. Certainly there were rough edges to his batting technique ... hardly surprising considering the poor facilities he had had to live with and the absence of any form of coaching. But the basic method was sound and the determination to succeed shone through. It was a two-day match, and on the first evening we, the whites that is, smuggled a cricket bag full of beer past a bevy of thinly disguised men from the 'Special Branch' who were there to make sure no contact and, by inference, contamination between the races took place. I recall to this day the expression of disbelief on Basil's face when I popped my head into their dressing room at the end of play to invite him and his team-mates into ours for a drink. In those days every white man was 'Mr' or 'Baas' (boss). 'Thank you, Baas' said Basil, and with a precautionary glance outside to see where the men in the lightweight brown suits and snapbrim hats had positioned themselves, he and a few of his team sidled in. It would be immodest to suggest that the half hour we cricketers had together splintered the barriers of South Africa's apartheid policy, but it did forge between Basil, myself and John Abrahams, another coloured cricketer who played in that Natalspruit game and who later followed Basil into Lancashire League cricket, a bond of friendship that has never since wavered.

It's often said that the best fighters are hungry fighters. If so, then Basil d'Oliveira's appetite for recognition in the cricketing world outside Cape Town gave England her most steadfast champion of the post-war period. His Test match record is an impressive one and grows in worth when taking into account the age (thirty-five) that he first played and the quality of the international opposition around at the time. Forty-four caps for England between 1966 and 1972, 2484 runs averaging 40.067, including two hundreds against

Australia and another against possibly the strongest representative team ever assembled, the Rest of the World in 1970. Throw in his 47 Test wickets plus 29 catches and you have one of the most significant individual contributions to English cricket since the end of the war. There was also that intangible feeling of stability he brought to an England team during a period of team rebuilding and erratic performances.

I cannot ever recall hearing of a game or a situation where d'Oliveira gave up trying. Most recently his heroic innings in the 1976 Benson and Hedges Cup final for Worcestershire against Kent captivated a full house at Lord's and the millions watching on television. The fact that Kent won quite comfortably by 42 runs is lost behind the memory of his innings of 50 played entirely on one leg after badly pulling a hamstring in the field during Kent's innings, an injury which robbed Worcestershire of their fifth and vital bowler. It was an innings of bravura and no little skill, built, I am sure, on the foundations of his long, hard struggle to rise above adversity in his youth in South Africa.

All sport, irrespective of the level it is played at, creates certain inner tensions, and jealousies. One player stands above this. One man who genuinely hasn't an enemy in the game. Basil Lewis d'Oliveira.

D'OLIVEIRA: Do you know, I can honestly say I have only one regret in life and that is that I didn't come to England sooner. It was like being reborn you know. I was too old really when I played first for Middleton in the Lancashire League in 1960. If I'd only played in England ten years earlier, who knows what might have been? Still, to have played 48 times for my adopted country is an honour I treasure above all others. Had it only been once, that would have been good enough.

WALKER: In those far-off days in South Africa in the 1950s it must have been desperately hard to get any form of recognition bearing in mind the limited opportunities you had for playing the game.

D'OLIVEIRA: If one grows up in a country like South Africa things are very black and white, if you'll pardon the pun! The law is very clear and no more so than in the area covering race relations. No integration. I used to play in our own non-European league in Cape Town and never thought I'd ever have the chance of playing on a grass wicket, let alone against whites. One of my first memories of good class cricket was as a boy watching the Australian Neil Harvey get a hundred at Newlands. That must have been round about 1950. I remember I cleaned out my father's pigeon loft every day for a week to earn the shilling I needed to get into the ground. But it was a long way from where we lived and so I didn't go to Newlands very often. But when I did have the chance to see good class cricket like the Currie Cup competition I found I had a good memory for players and their style. I never had any real coaching as a kid and I certainly haven't modelled myself on anyone. I've always tried to look at the best players and utilize their main gifts by grafting them on to my own style of play. What you learn with these (pointing at his eyes) stays with you a long time. What you learn with these (ears) doesn't often stay for long. I've always been a great believer in learning through watching. I'm still doing it now. When I first came to this country as the pro for Middleton I was really green, you know. I even had to be told that I must change in the same room as the rest of the players; man, I thought that as a professional and a coloured one at that I'd have to go behind a shed or something! But they made me feel so at home that this soon passed. The most difficult thing for me to adapt to was the changeover from matting to turf wickets. You see, I'd played virtually all my cricket at home on either a jute or coir mat stretched over gravel. The ball always bounced a predictable height. It also had consistent pace and the ball would certainly turn. Turf wickets are so much slower and unpredictable that for a long time I didn't think I'd ever succeed, and it's true I got pretty homesick at times, despite the greater personal freedom I had over here. But deep inside I knew that I *had* to make it because of everyone back in South Africa. For every ten people who wanted me to do well I also knew there were hundreds that were really hoping I'd fail, which would prove that I and therefore, by inference, the rest of South Africa's non-European cricketers weren't good enough. The extra responsibility of being the 'pro' in a Lancashire League team where you are expected to dominate with bat and ball was a pretty daunting experience, I can tell you.

Strangely enough, I found it a bit easier when I eventually joined Worcestershire in 1964. Sure, the standards were higher in every department, but the wickets were better, I was more experienced and therefore more confident in myself, and of course I was surrounded by ten other professionals, nearly all of whom were very competent performers.

WALKER: It didn't take you long to become one of the most vital cogs in a Worcestershire side which won the Championship in 1964 and 1965. Who impressed you in those early days?

D'OLIVEIRA: Tom Graveney. I've always thought him the finest specialist batsman I've ever played with or against. We shared in a lot of big partnerships for the county; Tom batting at 4, me at 5. He was such a good player on all kinds of wickets, and because he very rarely got bogged down he used to take the pressure off the rest of us because the scoreboard was always ticking over. He was such a beautiful batsman to watch too. There I'd be, short-arm jabbing away, fencing the ball off my body down to fine leg, and then 'elegant' Tom ... we always used to call him 'elegant' ... would get the strike and everything would change. When he was well set he had the capability of hitting two identical balls in absolutely opposite directions. I remember him at Hove once when John Snow was really roaring in down the hill. The first ball pitched just outside Tom's off stump – he had about 49 at the time – and away it went through the covers like a 303 bullet. Knowing 'Snowy', a bouncer was on the cards next ball. Instead he pitched it up in nearly the same place and Tom whipped it through mid-wicket with his

Take that!

feet in the identical spot to the ball before. That's great batting. He was also one of the few world-class players I've seen who played genuine quick bowling off the front foot; he even hooked with his weight on the left. At one stage of his career they didn't pick him for England because they said his temperament was suspect against the real quicks! But when the selectors were forced to bring him back in 1967 he got 257 at Nottingham against Roy Gilchrist and Co! But the thing that impressed me above everything else about Tom was his attitude to the game. He was just the same whether he got 0 or 100. He'd have a couple of pints in the bar at the end of the day's play and then start again in the morning. And of course he was an ideal professional model. He once told me that weather permitting he had a net every morning of the season! I always tell any kids that I might be coaching, if Tom Graveney needs ten minutes every day to keep in touch, lesser mortals like us need a couple of hours! He took net practice very seriously, none of this fooling around. He played in the nets just the same way as he did in the middle. He used to say to me: 'Bas, batting is just a series of habits. If you get into good ones when you're young, you're lucky. If you don't, then you've got to keep working at your game, just like a golfer. A top-class tournament professional wouldn't walk out onto the first tee without hitting forty or fifty balls on the practice ground. We're not any different.' It's this sort of application plus his philosophy that tomorrow's another day that I've tried to graft onto my own game.

WALKER: I've played against you many times and watched you from the ringside almost as often. What always impresses me is how simply you've reduced the problems of batting. You don't pick your bat up very high, so you don't have to come down far, nor do you let it wander off the straight. Even the way you build an innings, particularly during the first half an hour or so after you get to the crease, is pretty basic. You just don't take any chances. Is this a fair assessment?

D'OLIVEIRA: I would think so, yes. I'm lucky in that most of my strength is in my forearms. I don't need a very long armswing to generate power. This is why I favour the area through mid-wicket against the short-pitched delivery. With a bat movement of no more than a couple of feet I can hit it as hard as I ever need to. Against a fast bowler one hardly needs a back lift anyway, indeed it can be a disadvantage if he's truly quick. By not picking my bat up too far it helps cancel out any deviation from the straight when it comes down. I'm not the fastest man in the world on two legs, and being on the bulky side I've found through trial and error that providing I keep sideways on and get into line behind the ball I can make all the adjustments I need by using the strength and flexibility of my arms and wrists. But if I had to single out any one thing that I can be modestly proud about, it's my ability to concentrate. Perhaps it's because over the years I've had more incentive than most players to succeed! I like to define concentration quite simply as 'look at the ball'. It amazes me the number of well-known batsman who don't do just that. If you really look at the ball and don't take your eyes off it for an instant, that's concentration perfectly described. When I say this of course I'm assuming that the technical side of batting has become quite automatic through practice, but if anyone just sets out to watch the ball and nothing else, I'm prepared to bet a few pounds that his seasonal average will jump by at least ten runs per innings, and that's a lot. You have to concentrate as a bowler too, every bit as much. I believe, and I suppose you can apply this to batting as well, that you can only bowl one ball at a time. Concentrate on making that one ball the best possible.

WALKER: You've talked at length about Tom Graveney. Almost without exception everyone that I've talked to rates Gary Sobers as the greatest cricketer who ever lived.

D'OLIVEIRA: He was a genius. No doubt about it. We'll never see his like again. He could do everything ... and do it better than anyone else in the world. I'm so glad I played in the same era as Gary. You know, he was a humble person. Sure he used to play it as hard as hell on the field, but off it, a real nice guy. Never any 'agro' on the field. He'd beat you by backing his ability against yours, fair's fair. That's the way it ought to be. I'm afraid that this isn't always the case in the modern game. Perhaps there's too much money at stake, cricketers are getting too selfish. I know that great players, especially batsmen, are often accused of playing for themselves rather than the side. I never saw Gary do this.

WALKER: Have you?

D'OLIVEIRA: No, I've never played for Basil d'Oliveira in my life unless it's been in the interests of the side.

WALKER: Inevitably your name will always be linked with South Africa, the land of your birth, the land that refused to give you a chance when you were young, the land that refused to welcome an MCC team if you were included in it. As a result, South Africa was pushed into the cricketing wilderness and up until now, ten years later, there she still remains. In these circumstances, how do you feel about your homeland?

D'OLIVEIRA: If you're trying to suggest that I should feel bitter, well I don't. It was a traumatic experience to live through the events of 1968. You see, I thought I'd made the original touring team after scoring 158 against Australia in the final Test. Yes, I felt upset and bitter round about that time, but wouldn't you? It was going to be my chance to show the people back home that a coloured boy could make good in open competition, could live a decent, honest life without restrictions. Man, I was going to be the best behaved tourist the world's ever seen! But it wasn't to be, that is until I was drafted in as a late replacement for the injured Tommy Cartwright. The rest's history, and I don't think we need repeat it here. But I can say not going on that tour, if it had taken place, was the biggest disappointment of my life.

I've been back to South Africa many times since then to coach. I think we've all got a part to play in breaking down racial prejudice, wherever it might be, even right here in England. Lots of people have done a hell of a lot more than me and never had any credit for it ... even you and the rest of the lads with that game at Natalspruit opened the door another half inch. In 1968 and thereafter I think I made my point and won my own personal battle. They've been trying very hard to bring all the various cricketing bodies in South Africa under one umbrella and they've just succeeded. It's not proving an easy task to open up the sporting doors to men and women of all races, but they must continue to try, even though it may be too late. I've listened to people out there. There's a lot of dissatisfaction you know. You can't be registered as a black for five days and then an honorary white for the other two at the weekend when you're playing sport. When I go back I try to do my best to show that equality is a feasible proposition. Playing cricket in this country has certainly helped me to develop my confidence and to bring me out. I was so painfully shy and uncertain when I came to the UK fifteen-odd years ago. Now I feel relaxed in any company, and when I stop playing I hope to be able to stay in the game in a coaching capacity to help put back something into the game that has given me everything.

WALKER: Just how long can you go on for?

D'OLIVEIRA: Not long. These old legs are killing me. If you could get me a new bionic set, another ten years. I decided to call it a day at the end of the 1977 season but I've now agreed to soldier on for another season or two, although they better have a hospital bed ready for me! As the physio told me: 'Bas, it's just natural wear and tear.' The hardest part is the fielding. I can manage the batting but all this chasing around in the one-day competitions is no place for an old man like me. But life's been good. No, it's been bloody marvellous and I wouldn't have traded it for a different life ... not even for a new pair of legs!

Majid Khan

Great is a word bandied around in sport like a shuttlecock, but in reality there are very few cricketers who deserve the label. One I would suggest is Majid Jehangir Khan, former Glamorgan, Cambridge and now the leading Pakistan Test batsmen. If in sporting terms greatness can be defined as the ability to outplay all around you, then cricket must surely provide one of the most searching tests. Yet recognition of an individual's brilliance need not necessarily always shine in the spotlight of open competition.

At the windswept, icy county ground in Derby in 1969, Majid put on the most memorable exhibition of batting skill it has been my good fortune to personally witness. It took place in the Derbyshire nets during one of those seemingly endless breaks waiting for heavy overnight rain to drain through a waterlogged outfield. Huddled around the medieval dressing-room brazier thoughtfully provided by the Derby committee to combat the spine-chilling draughts that used to waft through the racecourse ground pavilion, the former headquarters of the county, the Glamorgan team's conversation turned to the art of batting. We had just come from a game against Sussex where Jim Parks Jnr had made a hundred against us on an unpredictable wicket. We agreed that it was the speed and precision of his footwork that had kept us, and Don Shepherd in particular, at bay. At that time, Shepherd was one of the country's most feared bowlers, a man of immaculate length and direction who bowled off-breaks at a brisk medium pace. On a turning wicket he was virtually unplayable, and touring teams in this country had gone away from games against Glamorgan at Swansea with a sigh of relief that the myopic England selectors did not include him in any of the Test sides.

While the discussion continued to and fro across the brazier, Majid, never at any stage of his career a talkative man, sat silent, orientally impassive. It was only when we had appeared to have exhausted all lines of debate that he spoke: 'You don't need any footwork in batting, just hands and eye.' In terms of length, this amounted to a major speech from Majid, then in his second season with Glamorgan, having joined on a special registration in 1968, the year after he had toured the UK with Pakistan. The Welsh county committee had no doubt been influenced in their signing of him, by his innings of 147 in eighty-nine minutes against Glamorgan at Swansea and the fact that his father, the distinguished Indian cricketer Dr Jehangir Khan, had been a pre-war Cambridge contemporary of Wilfred Wooller the Glamorgan secretary. These factors quickly helped to forge a bond which was to last until 1976.

At Derby on that bleak day in June 1969, Glamorgan were on the crest of a winning streak which lasted throughout the season, culminating in them taking the Championship for the second time in their first class history with an unbeaten record to boot, the first time this had been achieved since Lancashire in 1934. Success is a heady brew and there were many challengers to Majid's claim that footwork counted for nothing.

Within fifteen minutes, three of our front-line bowlers, including Don Shepherd, lined up in a net outside with Majid padded up at the other end about to have his theory demolished. For twenty minutes, on a rough, unprepared, and quite-impossible-to-bat-on wicket where the ball flew, shot, seamed and turned, Majid Khan stood absolutely motionless, parrying the ball as it lifted, cutting or hooking unerringly if it were wide, driving with frightening power if overpitched and swaying out of harm's way when it lifted unexpectedly.

Unless he allowed it, not a single ball passed his bat, not a chance was given, not a false stroke made. The bowlers were at full throttle, yet by our own critical reckoning afterwards that twenty-minute session must have yielded the young Pakistani around 75 runs! He had defied every known textbook instruction, improvised strokes that just did not exist and without uttering a word had emphatically made his point. In the presence of genius, no rules apply.

Of course Majid reproduced his skills in the middle too. His 156 against Worcestershire in the penultimate match of the 1969 season clinched the Championship for Glamorgan. That accurate county slow left-hander Doug Slade bowled four overs, 0-36 (9 x 4s), this on a helpful pitch! Majid's 109 in the Prudential Cup match against England at Trent Bridge in 1974 was an innings so brilliant and all-dominating that commentators and press critics ran out of superlatives.

Totally in control and ruthless in execution at the crease, Majid's character off the field could hardly be more diffident or less flamboyant. It took three long seasons in the United Kingdom before the unemotional man behind the inscrutable mask peeped out into the open. There's no question in my mind that it was his decision in 1970 to follow in his father's footsteps by going to Emmanuel College, Cambridge, that broke the ice. For the first time he felt truly comfortable in the Western world and in the informal, classless atmosphere at Cambridge the thaw at last began.

Despite his rather haphazard casual gait about the field, which gives the impression of his being somewhat bored with the proceedings, the inner core of the man who is now his country's leading opening batsman is one of steel. A man of absolutely rigid Muslim principles, throughout his eight years in the United Kingdom he never ever became fully assimilated into the free-wheeling loosely constructed freemasonry life of the professional county cricketer.

His four-year reign as captain of Glamorgan was considerably longer than that as leader of Pakistan. He proved that being a marvellous player does not automatically mean that similar inspirational juices flow as a director of tactics. Majid is too insular, too remote a man for this job, and his detachedness sadly inevitably led to a sordid and unpleasant end to his career as captain of Glamorgan and then player in August 1976.

He had had for him a disappointing season, plagued by an extended attack of hay fever which in turn set up an irritation behind the contact lenses which he has worn since 1971. At times his vision was so blurred that he could not focus clearly on anything further than five feet away. Yet he still managed 645 runs that year with a highest score of 204! Since the trouble cleared up he has batted with distinction against Lillee and Thomson in Australia and the battery of West Indian fast bowlers in the Caribbean, proving that the relative trickle in the cascade of runs that year was thankfully temporary.

But to back-track for a moment. After a series of palace intrigues in the Principality during the summer of 1976, Majid first resigned the captaincy of Glamorgan, complaining of secretarial and committee interference in the way he was leading the side, and then two weeks later asked not to be considered as a player for the remainder of the season because of what he described as a conspiracy against him by a number of senior players. So he left Wales, revered by all who had seen him play and admired in many quarters for his deep personal convictions.

It was this aspect of the man that interested me most as for five years as county colleagues we travelled the length and breadth of England. Besides his world-class abilities as a batsman, Majid was a first-class slip fielder and no mean bowler. Indeed, before he suffered a back injury which meant many years of sleeping on the floor or on boards under the mattress, he had been ranked as one of the fastest bowlers in the subcontinent. His first-class debut at the age of just fifteen gave an illustration of what was to come; 111 not out and six for 67! He made his Test debut at eighteen years and twenty-six days against Australia in Karachi in 1964, putting

Majid, the inscrutable Oriental

. . . but electrifying to watch, if you dare

him in the top ten youngest men ever to play Test cricket. One of *Wisden*'s 'Five Cricketers of the Year' in 1969, there are few honours that have not come his way.

Yet he remains the man least conscious of records and personal kudos that I've ever met. The few moments after a batsman returns to the pavilion after being dismissed are often the time when the air turns blue! Majid had played for Glamorgan for three seasons before I heard the first 'swear' word pass his lips – a *sotto voce* 'damn'!

Long hours in the field together, side by side at first and second slip, saw our between-ball conversations range over an enormous area ... religion, colour prejudice, Eastern footwear, Western morals, Pakistani attitudes, Indian history, etc., etc. Alone, as we sat at railway stations, strolled around a boundary edge eating ice-creams – at which he is the British all-comers record-holder – the thoughts and aspirations of this introvert gradually emerged. During the 1971 season we sat, each eating a cornet – my first, his fourth – watching our colleagues bat at Chesterfield in Derbyshire, one of the loveliest grounds in all Christendom. We talked of this and that.

WALKER: One thing which has always intrigued me about you Majid is why you ever decided to become a professional cricketer. I've seen for myself your home background; in this country it could certainly come into the 'upper-class' bracket and the whole concept of playing for money seems to me anyway a complete rejection of the type of life which fate would have cut out for you at home in Pakistan.

MAJID: There was initially, I agree, a certain antagonism towards professional cricketers at home. Mustaq Mohammed was the first international player from my country to break the ice, then Asif Iqbal, and I after the 1967 tour here. Now we have Sarfraz, Intikhab, Younis, Zahir and Sadiq all involved with English counties and we are gradually being accepted at home. More will surely follow. Funnily enough, my family never tried to influence me against turning pro;

though an uncle did once say: 'Get a degree first.' I've been lucky. I'm managing to combine both an academic and sporting life at the moment. I suppose the decision by Asif to join Kent and myself to go to Glamorgan has started something of a snowball. Now most of the Pakistan international team would like to play county cricket. I would like to continue playing for Glamorgan at least until I'm thirty, and possibly beyond, but of course if and when I get married I'll have to review the position. As you know our marriages are arranged by our parents but I have told them that my wife must be prepared to give me my cricketing wishes until I'm thirty, then we shall look at the pattern of the future together.

WALKER: Having been personally associated with you over the past three seasons, I've seen you play at least ten innings which I would humbly bow to as true cricketing genius. Your method and technique have that individual flair and radiance which temporarily reduces all other cricketers around you to the role of selling-platers. Yet I have never played with such an outwardly unexcitable or unemotional person. Do you think this serenity has anything to do with your success?

MAJID: I have always kept my emotions bottled up and well under control. I have been like this ever since I can remember. I think I take after my father in this respect. I have a very simple philosophy both in cricket and life. I believe that God knows best. As a Muslim I know that if I fail and fail again and again, on or off the field, it is because He wills it. God knows what is good for me. If I make nought or play a bad shot and get out I am irritated and depressed for five or ten minutes afterwards but then it's over. I never brood or fret. I get a little nervous before I go in, but I prefer not to watch the batsmen before me at work. It might give me a preconceived idea as to how the wicket is playing and if the bowler is on form. Far too much cricket is played in the minds of those in the dressing-room and it's usually negative in content. I believe in playing each ball, each game, on the merit of the moment.

WALKER: You really are a remarkably phlegmatic person. I remember one innings of yours in 1969 against Worcester at Cardiff; you scored 156, which won us the game and the County Championship. Before it, you sat in a far corner of the dressing room with your head resting on your bat handle and we had to shake you to tell you a wicket had fallen and you were in. Of those runs, 114 were scored before lunch on a 'raving turner' against Gifford, Slade, d'Oliveira and Holder – an innings of complete domination.

MAJID: Thank you, Peter. I do remember that innings, but I'm sure there are several overseas players who could have done just the same; people like Procter, Sobers, Richards and Lloyd. You see, I believe that the British are the least 'ball-conscious' nation I know. Most 'foreigners' have far greater natural ability but lack the discipline and hard work which are the British sportsman's main qualities. In cricket, many of the attacking batsmen from overseas rely very little on extensive footwork; the complete opposite of Boycott for instance, who is technically as near perfect as one can humanly expect but who because of this has enchained himself inside very limited scoring arcs if the bowling is accurate. Like the batsmen I mentioned earlier, I rely principally on my eyes, arms and wrists. In the 1950s, May, Graveney and Cowdrey played more like we do; the modern English Test batsman seems to have lost this quality. Also, most of us from overseas score primarily from off the back foot. There's a much bigger variety of strokes there than on the front foot. By lunging forward as the first movement one's scoring range is severely cut down, but on the back foot one can improvise so much more. If your wrists are in control you can hit firmly from off the front foot even though one's initial movement was back.

WALKER: What made you decide to join Glamorgan? After all, you must have had many offers as the 1967 tour drew to a close.

MAJID: Well, actually I didn't. After my 147 at Swansea, Wilf Wooller, the Glamorgan secretary who had been at

Cambridge with my father, asked me if I would like to join the club. I said yes but that I would like time to think it over and to consider any other offers. Somehow it was leaked to the press that I was on the point of signing for Glamorgan, so of course the other counties didn't bother! Looking back I'm very pleased they didn't, because I'm really very happy playing for Glamorgan. I've found the Welsh far more hospitable and friendly than the English. Also Glamorgan are a happy side – no backbiting, everyone trying for the team. I must play in a collectively happy side like this one or the recent Cambridge team, otherwise I just don't want to play. Cricket is the most important thing in the physical part of my life so the conditions must be of my own choosing.

WALKER: Although you're generally recognized by those who play with and against you as a batsman of the very highest class, your Test record to date has led critics to suggest that you lack that small indefinable something which would give you their unconditional stamp of being a great player. Are you aware of this apparent failing?

MAJID: Not really. Always remember that although I made my Test debut in 1964, I've only played in twelve Tests. But really I'm sure the reason behind my comparatively moderate Test record lies in my answer to your previous question – I must play in a happy side for me to produce my best. Draw your own conclusions. Until I turned professional I only played two or three first-class games a year, just like all the other Pakistan cricketers – really we come into the international scene merely as goodish club players. Compare the amount of cricket I've played with, say, the career of Alan Knott who played his first Test as recently as 1967 yet he's already appeared in more than thirty Tests! Also I suppose I do lack the 'killer instinct' of the truly great player; after I get to a hundred I often throw it away.

WALKER: You played in two of the three Tests against England this summer. How highly do you rate the present Pakistan side?

MAJID: In my mind there is no doubt that with the right

organization behind the scenes, this current crop of players and those coming up could make Pakistan one of the strongest cricketing powers in the world. I'm a very patriotic man. I want to see my country develop, not just materially but morally as well. We need strong, decisive leadership from the Board of Control in Pakistan. We need to play more cricket of a first-class nature, say in a Sheffild Shield type of competition. I would also like to see us resume fixtures against India. The last time we met was in 1961, but I can assure you that the players on both sides are eager and willing to start a Test series again. Naturally I am disappointed that the MCC tour to my country is likely to be postponed .for twelve months because of internal political difficulties in Pakistan, but I sympathize and understand the cricketing authorities' attitude in the United Kingdom. They must ensure the safety of their players as their number one priority, but if the tour is off, it will be a big blow to cricket lovers at home. Our game thrives on touring teams, and we see so little of the world's best players that a postponement of this type will be hard to bear.

WALKER: With your background and experience of leadership at Cambridge I would like to suggest you'd make a fine future captain of Pakistan. Does this idea appeal to you?

MAJID: Of course, yes. What young player in my position would say otherwise? However this is not a decision for me to make. But on a broader aspect, I can see a much more telling long-term contribution being made by myself and others like Wasim, Pervez and Asif after we stop playing, in the future administration and organization of the game in Pakistan. I think we could be a world force in five years.

WALKER: Has life in this country in any way changed you?

MAJID: The biggest ifluence on me during my three years' stay has unquestionably been my time at Cambridge. In human terms I'm a lot more tolerant of other people's ideas and beliefs, and it's largely removed the elements of class distinction which were strongly ingrained in me through my Pakistani background. I've made some fine friends at University, particularly Gerald Davies, the British Lions rugby player who has just finished doing an English literature degree at Emmanuel College, and Phil Edmonds from Zambia, who I believe has world-class potential as a slow left-hand bowler. In cricketing terms, as captain I've tried to 'harden' the normally casual University attitude to cricket and I think reasonably successfully at that. Our record this year shows we can compete on equal terms and even beat some first-class counties like Sussex and Leicester, and of course we beat Pakistan! Captaincy has made me a better player. Certainly my defence has improved knowing that the success of the Cambridge team largely depends on my own contribution with the bat. The life there has also helped my concentration; no captain can afford to switch off mentally. I find it is much easier to come back into county cricket and a good side like Glamorgan because the pressure is less. I so enjoy both the standard of play and the companionship within the Welsh club that I would like to remain here for many years to come and help to keep cricket alive in this county – a sentiment and aspiration I share incidentally with all my Glamorgan colleagues.

Brian Close

If ever I needed to answer an allegation that today's professional cricket lacks characters, my defence plea would be: 'Call Brian Close.' Remarkable is an inadequate word to describe this larger-than-life personality. From such stuff are forged tail-gunners, free-fall parachutists and bullfighters. Close epitomizes all that is tough, uncompromising and bigoted about cricket, and Yorkshire cricketers in particular.

Although he played the last seven years of his first-class career, which began in 1949, with Somerset, Close remained as Yorkshire as their pud. On occasions his critics would say he was as thick and indigestible as a bad example of that county's best-known delicacy. The streak of obstinacy that runs through all successful games players, and in particular those from the northern parts of England, is certainly broad down the ample back of Brian Close, at eighteen years and 149 days the youngest man ever to play Test cricket for England. His single-minded total belief in his own cricketing infallibility is one reason why he survived so long in a game which at professional level often ages and dispirits more than it uplifts. But whatever his failings, it's impossible not to be impressed by the Yorkshireman's courage and willingness to lead by personal example.

Nowhere was this better demonstrated than in the Lord's Test match against the West Indies in 1963. There he challenged in just about the nearest thing one can get in cricket

Close: a living legend

to single-handed combat Wes Hall and Charlie Griffiths, the West Indies fast bowlers. It cannot be called either a fair or an unarmed fight because a 5½-oz rock-hard cricket ball in the hands of those two fast bowlers carried as much lethal potential as David's slingshot! Pictures of Close's black-and-blue body after his innings of 70 in the second innings of the Test which has gone into history as 'Cowdrey's match' have lasted longer in the memory of his fellow players than the more dramatic shots of Colin's broken arm encased in plaster coming out to join David Allen, who had to face the last over of the match from Hall to save the game for England. It is innings like this which ensure that the name of Brian Close, even in his retirement, lives on wherever the game is played in the United Kingdom.

Close is a large man; six feet two inches in height with a deep chest and shoulders which would be the envy of many a heavyweight boxer. The strain of carrying such a powerful superstructure through literally thousands of hours in the field and his full-time involvement as an all-rounder who has scored 35,000 runs, taken nearly 1200 wickets and held 800 catches have taken their inevitable toll, so that when he got injured at all in the latter part of his career it was usually in the legs. He's a man with a high pain threshold. Fielding as he did a mere two to three yards from the bat he needed to be. He took some fearful cracks, some of which have gone into cricketing folklore. Like the time a county batsman connected with a full-blooded pull smacking Close at short square leg on the side of the head. The ball rebounded in a high parabola to mid-wicket, where it was caught. Everyone rushed to see if the great man was still alive. He stood there unmoved and unbloodied. Relieved that he had not after all been struck a fatal blow, one of his team mates said: 'Bloody hell, you were lucky, Closey, but what would have happened if it had struck you between the eyes?' 'He'd have been caught at cover' was Close's dismissive reply. And he meant it!

Close is still a remarkable athlete. A fine soccer player before knee trouble and his increasing cricket commitments forced him out of the game, he also is a golfer of no mean skill, playing off a handicap of 3 right-handed and 8 left! Fred Trueman tells a marvellous story of a round with Brian during their Yorkshire days together. As in everything sporting, Close likes to win. But on this occasion little was going right. He hooked and sliced his way around the course until their fourball reached the twelfth, a dogleg to the right around a lake. After slicing two balls from the tee straight into irretrievable water, Brian yanked out a left-hand driver. His anger knew no bounds as, aiming far away out of trouble, he hooked his third ball way out into the middle of the lake. It's not often that Brian Close is silent, but according to Fred Trueman, without a word he picked up his bag and trolley, walked six yards to the water's edge, and from high over his head hurled both far out into the deep. He then turned and stalked back towards the distant clubhouse, leaving Fred and the others to continue their round as a threesome. Imagine their surprise when playing the thirteenth, which came back down the other side of the lake, at the appearance of the husky but somewhat chastened figure of Close returning towards them. 'I thought he was coming back to apologize,' remembers Fred, 'but I ought to have known Closey better. He passed us muttering: "Can't get back to t' bloody hotel; left car keys in t' golf bag!"' Their last sight of him that day was of the then England all-rounder waist deep in slimy green water fishing around with his bare feet in the approximate position his bag had sunk from sight!

Brian Close never accepted authority without question, though he expected his own to be unchallenged. This stubbornness, together with an inability to hold his tongue on occasions, cost him the captaincy of England after an incident involving a spectator at Birmingham when he was still skipper of Yorkshire. But this outspokenness remains one of his most endearing charms, for Close speaks directly and squarely about Close and the game of cricket as he sees it.

He spent twenty-nine years in first-class cricket, twenty-two of them with his native Yorkshire, and until his retirement at the end of the 1977 season he was one of the few contemporary cricketers who had played with and against men known to today's performers only as legends from the past ... Lindwall, Miller, Hutton, Compton, Weekes *et al.* Because of this he was enormously conscious of the traditions and the ongoing heritage that he represented. To him the game of cricket was as important and as dear as life itself.

My own recollections of playing against Brian Close are vivid. Memories of the balding pate, the huge forehead and beetle eyebrows underneath with two intense light blue eyes glaring at me when batting still make me sit up in bed with a start during a restless night!

The great forward lunge which characterized his own early sparrings at the batting crease challenged the quicker bowlers to dig it in short, aiming to hit his body. He was never lacking in courage. As a bowler he was known as 'the man with the golden arm' because of his extraordinary luck in getting wickets with rank bad balls. And as an international captain I believe he was responsible for the re-emergence of English pride and determination during the last decade. This became particularly apparent under Illingworth and Greig, two self-confessed admirers of Close. All three often led teams who played a great deal of tight, disciplined cricket against very much more talented opposition.

The recall of Brian Close, then forty-five, to the England Test team in 1976 as an opener to blunt the ferocity of West Indian fast bowlers Holding, Roberts and Daniel is one of cricket's more endearing fairy stories. The batting of Close and John Edrich, another veteran, in the second innings of the Old Trafford Test match must rank as one of the most outstanding examples of sheer guts ever recorded in sport. On a brute of a wicket, Edrich and Close – who took the bulk of the lightning-fast Holding – stood firm without a backward step. Close, who never believed in showing an opponent that he'd been hurt, did once momentarily buckle at the knees after being struck in the pit of the stomach by Holding. It was the first time in his career that anyone could recall his registering pain, but he was right behind the ball next delivery! In the dressing room at the end of the day's play after he and Close had survived ninety minutes against three fast bowlers out more to maim than to remove them, John Edrich (not a man renowned for either the lavishness or frequency of his praise) said after Close had disappeared into the warm, soothing embrace of a bath: 'Watching that guy play out there this evening made me proud to be an Englishman.'

He and Close were dropped for the next Test!

These exchanges between Brian Close and myself are an amalgam of several years' conversations. I think they reveal him for what he was and still is, a committed, totally dedicated man who believes in the divinity of cricket and his own place at the right hand of the Great Umpire.

WALKER: To me you've always epitomized the legendary uncompromisingly tough-as-old-boots type of Yorkshire cricketer, absolutely obsessed by the game, single-minded in pursuit of victory, contemptuous of failure and with a total belief in your own and your side's supremacy. When you moved into south-western England and the softer, or if I can put it this way, kinder, more compassionate atmosphere that exists in Somerset, was it a difficult adjustment for you to make?

CLOSE: I agree with you that I play it hard, but after all isn't that what being a professional cricketer means? But on a personal level there was a difference in the way I approached a new season, even each new game, compared to the days when I belonged body and soul to Yorkshire. That club was my whole life. Everything I did was geared to the advantage and betterment of Yorkshire. Up there folk tend to call a shovel a bloody spade and I suppose there are more opinions and arguments going on at this very minute in Yorkshire about cricket than in the rest of the country put together. When I was sacked by the club at the end of the 1970 season for what were really trivial reasons – just a normal clash of personalities that have always been part and parcel of

Yorkshire cricket since the days of Lord Hawke – I just couldn't believe it. Twenty-two years I'd been with them, and for months afterwards I felt as if I'd been anaesthetized. Even now, eight years since the event, I can't understand why it should have happened.

WALKER: Do you still feel resentful about the way things were handled by the Yorkshire committee?

CLOSE: It's not only elephants that don't forget, Peter lad. But no, not really. After all, time does mellow even the blackest sections of the memory. But one thing still rankles. I can't forget, or forgive, the sort of personal accusations made by certain members of the Yorkshire committee about my behaviour off the field. I challenged them to a 'face-to-face' confrontation on television to give me a chance to reply to them, but they refused. Committees are pretty much the same wherever you go, I'm afraid, and this applies to other sports, not just cricket. What still hurts is that millions of people who don't know me except through the press and television think as a result of that upheaval that I am some kind of monster. I may look like that to some out on the field, but of course I'm not at all like that.

WALKER: What were your feelings, then, when you returned to play in Yorkshire as captain of Somerset, a county that you must always have fancied as a bit of a soft touch when you were leading Yorkshire?

CLOSE: It was all right after a while. The crowd wanted me to do well, I think ... there were a lot of people who didn't want me to leave, you know. What I do remember and remember quite vividly was my first visit to Headingley after I'd been sacked. It was during the next season, 1971, the third Test against Pakistan. I stood in the crowd at the back of the public bank and felt terrible. I was so embarrassed. I didn't feel at all at home until after the game when I went into the bar the players use and spoke to the lads there. That wasn't too bad, but I don't want to go through another day like that, thank you.

WALKER: For so much of the latter part of your career

'England expects. . .'

you were in charge of a team – Yorkshire, England and then Somerset. But in 1971, the first year for your adopted county, you played under the captaincy of Brian Langford. How did you adjust to being just another member of a team?

CLOSE: I must admit it was difficult. The transition took me most of that first season, but I enjoyed it. The pressures of captaining a side like Yorkshire aren't like anything else in cricket. Up there they expect success as a natural birthright and you must dominate, grind the opposition into the ground and win decisively. But I admit it's different these days from when I started. Then there were some very hard-assed men around and often the real battle on the field would be amongst the Yorkshire players themselves; the opposing batsmen were just blown out of the way as an afterthought! A lot of good, no, a lot of great sides are like this. Real nigglers. Surrey in the 1950s for example. I don't altogether go along with the theory that a happy dressing-room atmosphere automatically gives a side a better chance of success. Like in boxing, you need mean and hungry fighters, ten men jealous of a team-mate's achievements and each wanting to do a little bit better.

At Somerset they're not used to extended periods of success, so a convincing win is a bit like a Christmas bonus. Being a single cog in a team again gave me a chance to have a fresh look at my own game and I think that one season as an ordinary playing member helped in my continuing in the game as long as I did. Few people, even those closely connected with cricket, fully appreciate the strain in leading a county side seven days a week in the various competitions we play in these days. It really tells. Many cricketers, and in particular captains, find the whole thing building up off the field, putting enormous pressures on personal and family life. It affected me too. I can't begin to think of how many cups of 3 a.m. tea I've made when I haven't been able to sleep because of an aspect of the game which is worrying me; either the way it's going or perhaps an emotional concern about one of the players. I've really scraped the barrel of nervous tension, lad. Yorkshire in the Sixties were a team full of strong personalities: they weren't easy to weld together, but what a fine side they were. Funnily enough, although I always wanted to end my days as an ordinary player – for Yorkshire ideally, to be realistic – it only took just that one season in the ranks with Somerset to whet the old appetite to get back in control again. I'm particularly pleased with the way we've performed in the limited-over competitions recently. In 1976 we should have won the John Player Sunday League but for a freak loss at Cardiff against Glamorgan in the final match of the season. If we played that game again another ten times, we'd win all ten. But that's half the charm of our great game, and personally I think I've confounded people who in the past castigated me for my criticisms about limited-over cricket.

WALKER: Come, come, Brian. Be fair. Yours was one of the earliest and certainly the loudest voice raised in criticism of this kind of cricket when it really took off in 1969 with the start of the Sunday League. By then the Gillette Cup was already six years old and now we have the Benson & Hedges competition, not forgetting the Prudential Cup at international level. Has your own and Somerset's success in recent years mellowed your attitude at all?

CLOSE: No, I wouldn't say it has. Indeed I'm now more convinced than ever that my original reservations still stand. To me the basis of cricket is attacking bowling backed by aggressive fielding. In the Sunday League in particular, both these aspects of the game are approached from the negative point of view; the bowler tries to bowl a ball not to be hit and doesn't really look to get anyone out, while the fielders are concerned with saving runs. It's the sort of game which encourages a top-class batsman to make a fool of himself trying to break out of the stranglehold. No youngster or middle-order player will ever establish himself or improve his technique with this sort of limitation. In limited-over cricket the conditions and rules of the game dictate the attitude of the players instead of, as I believe, the other way round. A cricketer should have the space and time to express his own personality. Forty overs is only a Sunday knockabout entertainment, a comedy played seriously; it's certainly not 'first class', and I think it's time we put it into its right perspective.

The public are now beginning to appreciate that it's a gimmick, and in my view it's done great damage to the up-and-coming youngsters who are our cricketing future. I think that limited-over cricket generally has had a lot to do with the decline in English standards in the 1970s. It's not just sour grapes, because I proved I could still play it as well as anyone, but when I skippered Yorkshire I used to hate running the game on Sundays. After spending all week trying to get our players thinking positively, on the seventh day I then had to ask them to do almost everything against the cricketing commonsense I'd been preaching for the previous six!

I believe it's destroyed the stability of players and created false tensions and false attitudes, particularly in the minds of newcomers. Having said my piece about the playing aspects, I do appreciate we need the commercial sponsorship to keep first-class cricket alive in this country. But that doesn't mean to say I believe wholeheartedly in the product I have to sell.

WALKER: How then do you see today's game? Are you equally pessimistic about the future of the three-day contest if limited-over cricket is having such a bad overall effect on standards?

CLOSE: Well, the sponsorship of the County Championship by Schweppes will ease the financial problems a great deal in the short term, and after all we've got money in the bank after the two recent glorious summers with the Prudential Cup and the entertaining West Indies here. But speaking purely on the cricketing side, I would like to see part-time players engaged in one three-day game a week staged over the weekend. Let's cut back on the gimmicks and get back to playing the real stuff which produces top-class Test cricketers. Also I don't agree with us having so many overseas players in the United Kingdom game. The new registration laws will help, though, by limiting each county to no more than two members of their side not qualified for England. I've a great respect and liking for many of the overseas lads, but I don't believe they care for the future of English cricket as I do. Also, if we have the best overseas players in the world taking part in our County Championship, then when they appear with their own countries here on tour it cheapens the whole impact of Test cricket.

I'm also convinced that a lot of modern captaincy leaves much to be desired. When I began, slow bowlers did the donkey work. Now it's the medium-pacer, banging away short of a length to his captain's negative defensive field, and the whole tone of the game is geared towards saving rather than winning matches. I do believe most emphatically that there is too much pressure on first-class players for the good of the game. Complicated scoring systems, widely different competitions, and above all the enormous distances they have to travel each season all contribute towards the lessening of a first-class cricketer's motivation and certainly adversely affect his keenness. It's not surprising that performances fluctuate so wildly. Hell, you can't even scratch your arse without having it endlessly analysed on slow-motion action replay! To me the game isn't so satisfying today as it was when I started in the late Forties. Now it tends to blunt one mentally rather than stimulate as it used to. But if we go back to basics, I mean the simple contest between bat and ball, we won't be far wrong. That's the real charm and lasting quality of cricket.

WALKER: What in your view makes a good captain?

CLOSE: You've got to lead from the front. Gone are the days when you were given your place and position simply because you had a double-barrelled name and a university education. You need flair and the ability to take individual decisions even when the consensus of team opinion is against you. Occasionally you have to be able to live the life of the loner. England have had an odd mixture of captains since I was in control. Ray Illingworth. Now he played under me for years when we were in the Yorkshire side, and he's got many fine qualities but not, I suspect, the ability to read the Riot Act when it matters or to create enough enthusiasm inside the team. You've got to be a bit of an exhibitionist, you know – being flamboyant, like Richie Benaud for example, often helps to kid the opposition, take it from me. But for a couple of years Ray did a fine job leading a not very good England team, and if he's to be judged by his record then he must be rated one of our most successful captains.

Tony Lewis? Well he was here today, gone tomorrow, and he's another one who found the pressure of county captaincy too much, resigning from the leadership of Glamorgan while skippering the MCC in India.

Mike Denness? The oddest of all, unquestionably. Never quite good enough as a player and made too many tactical errors as a captain. At international level you've got to be worth your place as a performer pure and simple.

Tony Greig? Well, he's a highly talented if erratic cricketer, but when he led England he did wonders in jacking up morale when their spirits were really down. He's about the hardest trier I've met outside the Yorkshire Leagues, but although he came out smelling of roses after the recent tour to India, I don't think the selectors always gave him the right players. I was very disappointed when he chucked it all in for Packer's money; he'd have been captain of England for years. Mike Brearley did marvellously well against, admittedly, a dreadful Australian side in 1977 and he did win the Ashes. But is he a good enough player to survive as captain?

WALKER: Like Tennyson's brook, Brian, you looked as if you could have gone on playing for ever. What happened?

CLOSE: At the start of 1977 I really felt that I could play for another couple of seasons, but then I had a bad attack of bronchitis early in May and was never ever fully fit after that. At a professional level cricket is such a physically taxing sport, particularly for a captain, that there was no way in which I could take the field and make the sort of contribution I would demand from myself. I know it's often said, 'once a Tyke, always a Tyke', but after I left Yorkshire my loyalties and ambitions were completely those of Somerset. The current lot of players are a great bunch of lads and in Viv Richards we have one of the best, if not the best, batsman in the world. But I struggled whenever I got on to the field during 1977. The fielding was bloody murder, also the running between the wickets. We play in three limited-over competitions where you're at a fast gallop all the time, so I soon realized, with great regret, that I had to pack it all in.

WALKER: Now you're in a position to be a little more objective about the game, how do you interpret it?

CLOSE: There's not much difference these days between a side that does moderately well and one that wins a major competition. A lot of a team's success is to do with who's got the fiercest desire to win. Hell, I was competing against men ever since the age of eleven. I played professional football at fourteen, and during my last turbulent days at Yorkshire I even seriously thought of trying my hand on the professional golf circuit for six months. When I was playing first-class cricket I don't believe there was anyone who knew more about competition and what pressure means. Somerset can be one of England's premier clubs in the 1980s and I would have liked to be out there in the field helping them on the way. But it's not to be, though if I had managed to soldier on, one thing you could have been sure of – I'd have made bloody sure that the rest of the team were trying as hard as I was!